Mable Hoffman's CROCKERY COOKERY

Revised Edition

HPBOOKS

HPBooks
are published by
The Berkley Publishing Group
200 Madison Avenue
New York, NY 10016

Recipe development and testing: Mable Hoffman, Jan Robertson
Coauthors: Bill Fisher, Helen Fisher, Howard Fisher, Karen Fisher
Interior photography: Glenn Cormier

Book design by Richard Oriolo

Cover design by James R. Harris
Cover photo by George Kerrigan

First printing of revised edition: October 1995

Published simultaneously in Canada.

ISBN 1-55788-217-7

Printed in the United States of America

Acknowledgments

Special thanks to
Jan Robertson for her
invaluable assistance.

Contents

Introduction   1

Use & Care   3

Appetizers & Beverages   7

Soups & Sandwiches   25

Beef   55

Pork & Lamb   93

Poultry   117

Beans   155

Vegetables & Side Dishes   171

Breads & Cakes   199

Fruits & Desserts   217

Index   240

Introduction

 Welcome to the newest edition of *Crockery Cookery*. With over five million copies in print, this is the best-selling recipe book for slow cookers and one of the biggest-selling cookbooks of all time.

Since its introduction in 1975, *Crockery Cookery* has heralded the delicious, slow-cooking method. Cooks everywhere clamored for this book about the joys of slow cooking. As a result it became the #1 *New York Times* bestseller for thirteen weeks and was on best-selling charts for more than a year.

Cooking styles and eating habits are constantly changing. Now, more than ever, people are spending more time working and have less time to spend in the kitchen. Again the slow cooker comes to the rescue. Mable Hoffman brings you this newly revised edition reflecting the way we eat today. You'll find new flavor combinations, more herbs and spices, and less salt and fat.

You'll enjoy great new recipes such as Thai Chicken, Creole-Asian Strips, Red Beans & Rice, Lentil Casserole, Persimmon Pudding and more! Of course many traditional favorites have been kept, including Green Beans Portuguese Style, Cranberry Pork Roast, Soy-Glazed Spareribs and Apple Peanut Crumble.

Slow cooking is the secret of good cooks the world over. With a slow cooker you can enjoy the delicious simmered-in flavors of some of the world's best dishes without the time-consuming necessity of constant attention.

Whether you're cooking for one or two, or for many more, you can go to work or spend a day at leisure while your slow cooker gently mingles flavors and spices. Then you can return home to a piping-hot dinner that's ready to serve. It doesn't matter even if you're an hour or two late. It won't burn or taste overcooked. Dinner is ready when you are!

Superb and truly nourishing meals can be prepared with less expensive meats because slow cooking tenderizes in a special way that broiling or frying just can't duplicate. Meats are juicy and never cooked dry because slow cooking seals in the moisture. Farm-kitchen favorites such as stews and hearty soups simmer to perfection.

Slow cookers are also popular because they save time, money and energy. On a LOW setting, you'll be cooking with less energy than a 100-watt bulb. You can cook all day for only a few pennies—far less than the cost of cooking the same meal on your kitchen stove. You will also find that the slow cooker does not make your kitchen hot in the summertime.

Slow cooking is different and requires special recipes. The recipes in this book were developed specifically for slow cookers. Every recipe has been tested and retested to ensure your success with each meal you prepare. Within each chapter you will find a tantalizing variety of recipes so you can plan and serve meals to fit your tastes and preferences.

Welcome to the new world of slow cooking!

Use & Care

Slow Cooking

Low temperature is the success factor in slow cooking. Low heat and long cooking times help simmer flavor into food. It is best to use recipe times suggested in this book; however, if you cook longer, don't worry. Your food will not burn because it does not overheat.

Leave It Alone

The advantage of slow cooking is that you can set it and forget it because there is no need to watch the pot. Don't hesitate to leave your house to do what you want.

Stirring

Stirring is not required for recipes in this book or for slow cooking in general. Basting and brushing are needed for some recipes.

Keep It Covered

Leave the lid on. There is no need to keep looking at food as it simmers in a slow cooker. Steam and nutrients are trapped on the lid, condensed and returned to the cooking pot. This keeps food moist and nutritious even after cooking many hours. The steam atmosphere above the food helps cook from the top. Every time you take the lid off, the slow cooker loses steam. After you put the lid back on, it takes 15 to 20 minutes to regain the lost steam and temperature. Thus, taking the lid off means longer cooking times. *Never remove the lid during the first 2 hours when baking breads or cakes.*

Cooking Times

Until you become familiar with your slow cooker, follow the suggested recipe times. If you prefer softer vegetables or more well-done meat, cook longer than the indicated times.

Generally 1 hour on HIGH is equal to 2 hours on LOW.

Temperatures

Recipes in this book refer to two temperature settings, LOW and HIGH. LOW is 200F (93C) and HIGH is 300F (149C). Food in the slow cooker seldom gets hotter than 212F (100C).

High-Altitude Cooking

At high altitudes (over 4,000 feet), allow more time than given in the recipe. Whether you are using a slow cooker, stove or oven, food takes longer to cook at high altitudes.

At high altitudes, beans take about double the time given in the recipes. To reduce cooking time for beans, cover with water, bring to a boil in a pan on the stove, and simmer for 2 minutes. Let cool 1 hour. Or soak overnight. Return beans to slow cooker and proceed with the recipe.

Baking also requires longer cooking times at high altitudes.

Temperature Switches

Slow cookers generally have a three-position switch, OFF–LOW–HIGH. The switch snaps into the desired position as you turn it. You must snap this switch to LOW or HIGH to cook, not in between.

Spices

Because little evaporation takes place when cooking with your slow cooker, there are more juices when you finish than you would have with other cooking methods. For this reason you may want to increase the amount of spices you use in the recipes so they will suit your taste.

Frozen Foods

Frozen foods should be thawed before placing them in your slow cooker. Otherwise several extra hours must be added to the cooking time to compensate for the time required for the food to thaw before cooking actually begins.

Meat Rack

A metal meat rack or trivet will keep a roast out of juices and fats in the bottom of the cook pot and prevent the meat from sticking to the bottom.

Use a meat rack only when the recipes say to; it is not necessary or useful for all meats.

Baking

Baking requires a separate pan inside your slow cooker. The Breads & Cakes chapter suggests ways to use molds, coffee cans and other containers.

Before You Start Cooking

Wash the inside of your new slow cooker with soapy water. Do not immerse the slow cooker in water. Crockery, stoneware, Corning Ware, glass and nonstick surfaces may have a manufacturer's finished coating you can't see and don't want in your food. Washing removes it.

Cleaning Your Slow Cooker

Preventive maintenance and care will keep your slow cooker looking new. Don't allow food stains to burn into the finish. Soak the inside of the slow cooker with warm soapy water to loosen food, then scrub lightly with a plastic or nylon pad. Rinse well and dry. Slow cookers are now made of many different materials. Refer to manufacturer's instructions for cleaning.

Appetizers & Beverages

Think of your slow cooker as an extra helper when entertaining. Avoid the last-minute rushing about by starting several hours before a party. Combine the ingredients for one of the hot drinks, turn the control on the slow cooker to LOW, and the drink will be ready to serve when your guests arrive. What's more, it can be kept hot in a slow cooker without fear of scorching, boiling over or sticking to the pan. Perhaps you can borrow an extra slow cooker and have several silent helpers.

Cooking in a slow cooker is an especially good way to plan a get-together after the theater or ball game. You can plug in the slow cooker with ingredients for All-American Snack, then leave for the show. When you return with your friends, you can immediately offer them a hot snack and drink, or people can serve themselves whenever they are ready for refreshments.

For most of the beverage recipes, exact times are relatively unimportant. After several hours, the various fruit juices blend together for a smooth taste. However, if left on too many hours over the suggested time, they may become slightly bitter.

Relax and enjoy the festivities at your next party by letting your slow cooker keep your favorite appetizer hot. There is no reason for you to rush back and forth to the range or oven to serve hot snacks. Just heat them in a slow cooker. Have a group of small bowls and cups so guests can help themselves whenever they are ready for another serving. When you make Short-Cut Chili con Queso or Refried Bean Dip in a slow cooker, they will be the right consistency and temperature for all to enjoy.

For watching a game or viewing a special TV program, have spicy finger foods like Curried Almonds, Chili Nuts or East Indian Snack. Choose a fruity beverage like Spiced Apricot Punch or Tropical Tea. Holiday gatherings are the perfect occasions for Hot Spiced Burgundy or Bishop's Wine, and children too can join in sipping Hot Mint Malt or Padre Punch.

Mediterranean Caponata

Makes 6 to 8 servings

A variation of a traditional Sicilian recipe that may be served as a salad on lettuce-lined plates, or spread on crackers for an appetizer.

1 large eggplant, peeled and chopped
1 onion, chopped
2 plum tomatoes, peeled and chopped
1 tablespoon capers, drained
½ cup chopped celery
½ cup pimiento-stuffed green olives, chopped
1 clove garlic, crushed
2 tablespoons olive oil
1 tablespoon lemon juice
½ teaspoon salt
⅛ teaspoon pepper
6 to 8 anchovies, finely chopped (optional)
½ cup toasted pine nuts (see Note, below)

Combine eggplant, onion, tomatoes, capers, celery, olives, garlic, oil, lemon juice, salt and pepper in a slow cooker. Cover and cook on LOW 5 to 6 hours. Stir in anchovies, if using. Refrigerate 2 or 3 hours or until cool. Sprinkle with pine nuts.

NOTE: To toast pine nuts, heat in a 350F (175C) oven about 10 minutes or until golden brown.

Chicken & Leek Terrine

Makes 16 to 20 appetizers or 6 to 8 main-dish servings

When slicing a leek, use all the white part, plus the tender light-green section; discard the tough deep-green leaves.

1 lb. lean ground chicken or turkey
12 oz. bulk hot pork sausage
2 eggs, slightly beaten
¼ teaspoon dried marjoram
¼ teaspoon dried thyme
¼ teaspoon dried tarragon
½ teaspoon salt
⅛ teaspoon pepper
¼ cup dry white wine
1 tablespoon margarine or butter
1 small leek, thinly sliced
Crackers or toast rounds

In a large bowl, combine chicken, sausage, eggs, marjoram, thyme, tarragon, salt, pepper and wine. Set aside.

In a medium skillet, melt margarine or butter. Add sliced leek and sauté over medium heat until leek is limp. Place leek on bottom of a 6-cup mold or baking dish that fits into your slow cooker. Carefully spoon chicken mixture over leeks. Press lightly with the back of a spoon. Cover with foil.

Place a small metal rack in the bottom of the slow cooker; pour in 2 cups hot water. Set filled mold or baking dish on rack. Cover and cook on HIGH about 3 hours. Remove mold from pot. Leaving meat in the mold, cover and refrigerate several hours or overnight. Cut into wedges or thin slices. Serve with crackers or toast rounds.

Party-style Ratatouille

Makes about 4 cups

 Keep this warm in the slow cooker and let guests help themselves.

1 medium eggplant, peeled and finely chopped
1 zucchini, chopped
¼ cup sun-dried tomatoes in oil, drained and chopped
1 yellow bell pepper, finely chopped
1 medium red onion, finely chopped
1 clove garlic, crushed
¼ cup chopped fresh cilantro
3 tablespoons chopped fresh basil
2 tablespoons olive or vegetable oil
2 tablespoons white wine vinegar
½ teaspoon salt
¼ teaspoon pepper
Pita or sourdough rolls, cut into small wedges

Combine all ingredients except bread in a slow cooker. Cover and cook on LOW 6 to 7 hours or until vegetables are tender. Spoon on pita or sourdough wedges.

Short-Cut Chili con Queso
Makes about 4 cups

 A hearty, easy dip that's always a hit at potlucks or family get-togethers.

1 lb. pasteurized process cheese spread, cubed
1 (1-lb.) can chili without beans
4 green onions, finely chopped
1 (4-oz.) can diced green chiles, drained
Corn or tortilla chips

Combine cheese spread, chili, green onions and chiles in a slow cooker. Cover and heat on LOW 2 to 3 hours. Serve as a dip for corn or tortilla chips.

Refried Bean Dip
Makes about 3 cups

 An easy dip that requires just a few minutes preparation time—keep the slow cooker plugged in for a warm, self-serve appetizer.

1 (16-oz.) can refried beans
1 cup shredded Cheddar cheese
½ cup chopped green onions
2 tablespoons taco sauce
Tortilla or corn chips

In a slow cooker, combine beans, cheese, onions and taco sauce. Cover and heat on LOW 2 to 2½ hours. Use as a dip for tortilla or corn chips.

All-American Snack

Makes about 3 quarts

 Feel free to mix and match other cereals in the same amounts.

3 cups thin pretzel sticks
4 cups Wheat Chex cereal
4 cups Cheerios cereal
1 (13-oz.) can salted peanuts
1 teaspoon garlic salt
1 teaspoon celery salt
½ teaspoon seasoned salt
2 tablespoons grated Parmesan cheese
¼ cup margarine or butter, melted

In slow cooker, mix together pretzels, cereals, and peanuts. Sprinkle with garlic salt, celery salt, seasoned salt and cheese. Drizzle mixture with the margarine or butter and toss until well mixed. Cover and cook on LOW 3 to 4 hours. Uncover the last 30 to 40 minutes. Serve as an appetizer or snack.

East Indian Snack

Makes about 6 cups

Enjoy a snack that's just a little different; adjust the amount of curry powder to suit your taste.

1 (5-oz.) can crisp Chinese noodles
1½ cups (about 6 oz.) salted cashew nuts
2 cups Rice Chex cereal
½ cup flaked coconut
1 teaspoon curry powder
¼ teaspoon ground ginger
¼ cup margarine or butter, melted
1 tablespoon soy sauce

In slow cooker, mix together noodles, cashews, cereal and coconut. Sprinkle with curry and ginger. Add margarine or butter and soy sauce. Toss until well mixed. Cover and cook on LOW 3 to 4 hours. Uncover the last 30 to 40 minutes. Serve as appetizer or snack.

Chili Nuts

Makes about 5 cups

This spicy snack is just the thing for the next time you sit down to watch a television event. Have lots of cold drinks available, too.

2 (12-oz.) cans cocktail peanuts
¼ cup margarine or butter, melted
1 (1⅝-oz.) package chili seasoning mix

Add nuts to a slow cooker. Pour margarine or butter over nuts and sprinkle with dry chili mix. Toss until well mixed. Cover and heat on LOW 2 to 2½ hours. Turn control to HIGH, remove top, and cook on HIGH 10 or 15 minutes. Serve warm or cool in small nut dishes.

Curried Almonds

Makes about 3 cups

Each brand of curry powder is different. Try several and select your favorite blend.

2 tablespoons margarine or butter, melted
1 tablespoon curry powder
½ teaspoon seasoned salt
1 lb. blanched almonds

Combine margarine or butter with curry powder and seasoned salt in a medium bowl. Stir in almonds. Add to a slow cooker. Cover and cook on LOW 2 to 3 hours. Turn to HIGH, uncover, and cook on HIGH 1 to 1½ hours. Serve hot or cold, as a snack.

Spiced Apricot Punch
Makes 12 servings

 A harmonious blend of flavors, this beverage can be served from the pot.

1 (46-oz.) can apricot nectar
3 cups orange juice
¼ cup packed brown sugar

2 tablespoons fresh lemon juice
3 cinnamon sticks
½ teaspoon whole cloves

In a slow cooker, combine apricot nectar, orange juice, brown sugar and lemon juice. Tie cinnamon and cloves in a small cheesecloth bag; add to juices. Cover and heat on LOW 2 to 5 hours. Remove cheesecloth bag. Serve hot.

Cranberry Wine Punch
Makes 6 to 8 servings

 This deep crimson punch will add sparkle to any holiday occasion.

2 cups cranberry-raspberry juice
1 cup water
¾ cup sugar
1 (750-ml.) bottle Burgundy wine

1 lemon (unpeeled), thinly sliced
2 cinnamon sticks
6 whole cloves

Combine juice, water, sugar, wine and lemon in a slow cooker. Tie cinnamon and cloves in a small cheesecloth bag; add to cooker. Cover and heat on LOW 1 to 2 hours. Remove cheesecloth bag. Punch may be kept hot and served from slow cooker on the lowest setting.

Padre Punch

Makes 7 to 10 servings

A great flavor and golden amber color make this a very popular punch during the fall season.

1 (6-oz.) can frozen orange juice, partially thawed
3 orange juice cans of water
4 cups (1 quart) apple cider
1 teaspoon freshly grated nutmeg
¾ teaspoon ground ginger
2 cinnamon sticks
5 whole cloves
Orange slices

In a slow cooker, combine orange juice, water, cider, nutmeg and ginger. Tie cinnamon and cloves in a small cheesecloth bag; add to cooker. Cover and heat on LOW 4 to 6 hours. Remove cheesecloth bag. Garnish with orange slices. Keep hot and serve punch from slow cooker.

VARIATION: Recipe may be doubled if your slow cooker is large enough.

Hot Buttered Rum Punch

Makes 10 to 12 servings

 Add more or less rum, depending on your taste.

¾ cup packed brown sugar
4 cups water
¼ teaspoon salt
¼ teaspoon freshly grated nutmeg
½ teaspoon ground cinnamon
½ teaspoon ground allspice
¾ teaspoon ground cloves
2 (1-lb.) cans jellied cranberry sauce
4 cups (1 quart) pineapple juice
1 cup rum
Cinnamon sticks
Butter

In a slow cooker, combine brown sugar, water, salt, nutmeg, cinnamon, allspice and cloves. Break up cranberry sauce with a fork. Add cranberry sauce, pineapple juice and rum to cooker. Cover and heat on LOW 3 to 4 hours. Serve hot in individual mugs with cinnamon sticks. Dot each mug with butter.

Tropical Tea
Makes 10 servings

If your slow cooker is cold, warm it first with hot tap water so it won't crack when the boiling water is added.

6 tea bags
6 cups boiling water
⅓ cup sugar
2 tablespoons honey
1½ cups orange juice
1½ cups pineapple juice
1 orange (unpeeled), sliced
2 cinnamon sticks

Put tea bags into a slow cooker. Pour boiling water over tea bags; cover and let stand 5 minutes. Remove tea bags. Stir in sugar, honey, orange juice, pineapple juice, orange slices and cinnamon sticks. Cover and heat on LOW 2 to 3 hours. Serve from cooker.

Mulled Cider
Makes 10 to 12 servings

 A slow cooker keeps hot cider at the ideal temperature until you are ready to serve it.

2 quarts apple cider
¼ cup packed brown sugar
⅛ teaspoon ground ginger

1 orange (unpeeled), sliced
2 cinnamon sticks
1 teaspoon whole cloves

Combine cider, sugar, ginger and orange in a slow cooker. Tie cinnamon and cloves in a small cheesecloth bag; add to cooker. Cover and heat on LOW 2 to 5 hours. Remove cheesecloth bag. Serve from cooker.

Hot Mint Malt
Makes 6 servings

It's easy to produce a favorite chocolate mint drink in your slow cooker.

3 to 4 chocolate-covered, cream-filled mint patties (1½ inches in diameter)
5 cups milk
½ cup malted milk powder
1 teaspoon vanilla extract
Whipped cream

In a slow cooker, combine mint patties, milk, malted milk powder, and vanilla. Cover and heat on LOW 2 hours. Beat with a rotary beater until frothy. Pour into cups; top with whipped cream.

Spicy Tomato Juice Cocktail

Makes about 6 cups

 For additional spiciness, add a cup of salsa to this juice.

4 lbs. fresh tomatoes (12 to 14)
½ cup chopped celery
¼ cup chopped onion
2 tablespoons fresh lemon juice
1½ teaspoons sugar
½ teaspoon salt
1 teaspoon prepared horseradish
1 teaspoon Worcestershire sauce
⅛ teaspoon hot pepper sauce

Wash tomatoes; remove stem ends and cores. Remove seeds and chop tomatoes. In a slow cooker, combine tomatoes, celery and onion. Cover and cook on LOW 8 to 10 hours. Press through a food mill or sieve. Return juice to slow cooker. Cover and cook on HIGH 30 minutes. Add lemon juice, sugar, salt, horseradish, Worcestershire sauce and hot sauce. Cook on HIGH another 10 minutes. Cover and refrigerate until chilled.

Mediterranean Coffee
Makes 12 servings

This popular chocolate-coffee combination is further enhanced with spices and citrus flavors.

2 quarts strong hot coffee
¼ cup chocolate syrup
⅓ cup sugar
½ teaspoon anise flavoring (optional)
4 cinnamon sticks
1½ teaspoons whole cloves
Peel of 1 orange, in strips for twists
Peel of 1 lemon, in strips for twists
Whipped cream

Combine coffee, chocolate syrup, sugar, and anise, if using, in a slow cooker. Tie cinnamon and cloves in a small cheesecloth bag; add to cooker. Cover and cook on LOW 2 to 3 hours. Remove cheesecloth bag. Ladle coffee into cups. Add a twist of lemon peel, a twist of orange peel and a dollop of whipped cream to each cup.

Bishop's Wine

Makes 10 servings

 Put this together several hours ahead for flavors to blend together.

2 tablespoons whole cloves
3 oranges
2 (750-ml.) bottles dry red or white wine
½ cup sugar
1 cinnamon stick

Stick whole cloves into peel of oranges. Prick skin several times with a fork. Place in bottom of a slow cooker. Add wine, sugar and cinnamon. Cover and cook on LOW 3 to 4 hours. Serve hot from the cooker. If desired, cut oranges into wedges as a garnish for each serving.

Hot Spiced Burgundy
Makes 6 to 8 servings

Combine ingredients in your slow cooker and let flavors blend while you prepare accompanying treats.

2 tablespoons sugar
2 tablespoons fresh lemon juice
½ teaspoon freshly ground cinnamon
¼ teaspoon freshly grated nutmeg
½ cup hot water
1 (750-ml.) bottle Burgundy wine

In a slow cooker, combine sugar, lemon juice, cinnamon, nutmeg and water. Stir until well blended. Pour in wine, cover, and heat on LOW 2 to 2½ hours. Serve hot from the cooker.

Soups & Sandwiches

After you have tried some of my new soup recipes, you will be convinced that slow cookers were made just for this purpose. Zesty new flavor combinations and traditional favorites use a great variety of vegetables to make many of these hearty soups a true meal in a bowl.

If you are tired of rushing home after work or shopping to make dinner, plan to have a hearty main dish like Split-Pea Soup. Start with leftover turkey, chicken, or a ham bone. Then you can build almost any traditional soup with a few seasonings and vegetables. Put the ingredients into your slow cooker before you leave. When you get home, it will be ready to serve in large portions directly from the pot. To complete the meal, heat thick slices of buttered French bread. What could be easier?

Some soups are glamorous enough to serve to guests. Kilarney Chowder with sour cream added at the last minute is one example. Bouillabaisse, a French classic, is quite a conversation piece in itself.

Notice how the cooking times vary for these soups. Some take all day, and others can be prepared in an afternoon. Georgia Peanut Soup and

French Onion Soup are two faster recipes. Even so, at such low temperatures most soups are fine if they are cooked a little longer. At the minimum recommended cooking time, lift the lid and stick a fork into the meat and several of the larger vegetable pieces to test for doneness. Try not to keep the lid off any longer than necessary because steam and heat escape very fast. It takes a long time to replace the heat loss after you've replaced the lid.

Homemade or canned stock or broth work equally well in recipes that call for these ingredients.

Slow cookers work fine as serving pots for hot sandwiches. Sloppy Joes, Sloppy Jane Sandwiches and Chili Dogs will be the favorites for casual parties. You can combine the sandwich mixture in your slow cooker and leave it for several hours. Family members can serve themselves and make their own sandwiches or a group of friends can enjoy these hearty mixes after a game.

Fennel-Bean Soup

Makes 6 to 8 servings

When you trim the fennel, save a few small clusters of feathery leaves to sprinkle on each bowl of soup just before serving.

2 carrots, peeled and sliced ⅛ inch thick
1 small fennel bulb, trimmed and sliced
1 large onion, chopped
1 clove garlic, crushed
4 cups chicken broth
½ teaspoon salt
⅛ teaspoon pepper
1 (15-oz.) can cannellini beans (white kidney beans), undrained
2 cups coarsely shredded fresh spinach
Fennel leaves

In a slow cooker, combine carrots, fennel, onion, garlic, chicken broth, salt and pepper. Cover and cook on LOW 7 to 8 hours or until carrots are tender but not mushy. Turn control to HIGH. Add beans with liquid and shredded spinach. Cover and cook on HIGH 20 to 25 minutes. Spoon hot soup into large soup bowls. Top each with sprigs of fennel leaves.

Lentil Soup, Crescenti Style

Makes 8 servings

This is a large recipe—freeze half for a quick meal another day, if desired. This is a thick, hearty soup, similar to a stew.

1 to 2 lbs. beef neck bone or beef shanks
3 carrots, peeled and chopped
3 medium potatoes, peeled and chopped
1 large onion, peeled and chopped
3 celery stalks with tops, chopped
3 tomatoes, chopped
⅛ teaspoon dried marjoram
5 cups water
5 beef bouillon cubes, crumbled
½ lb. lentils
1 teaspoon salt
¼ teaspoon pepper
2 zucchini, chopped
½ small head cabbage, shredded

In a 4-quart or larger slow cooker, combine beef, carrots, potatoes, onion, celery, tomatoes, marjoram, water, bouillon cubes, lentils, salt and pepper. Cover and cook on LOW 9 to 10 hours or until lentils are tender. Remove beef bones from cooker; cut off meat and discard bones. Return meat to cooker. Turn control to HIGH. Add zucchini and cabbage, cover, and cook on HIGH 30 to 45 minutes or until vegetables are tender. Serve hot.

Potato Soup, Florentine Style

Makes about 6 servings

Thaw frozen spinach in a medium strainer over a large bowl, then press out excess water with the back of a large spoon.

4 medium potatoes, peeled and diced
1 onion, chopped
1 smoked ham hock (about 1 lb.) or 1 cup chopped ham
4 cups chicken broth
1 teaspoon dry mustard
½ teaspoon seasoned salt
⅛ teaspoon pepper
1 (9-oz.) package frozen chopped spinach, thawed and well drained
1 cup (4 oz.) shredded Jarlsberg or Swiss cheese

In a slow cooker, combine potatoes, onion, ham hock or ham, broth, mustard, seasoned salt and pepper. Cover and cook on LOW 7 to 8 hours or until potatoes are soft. Remove ham hock; chop meat and discard fat and bone. Return meat to cooker. Turn control to HIGH. Add drained spinach. Cover and cook on HIGH 15 to 20 minutes. Spoon hot soup into soup bowls and sprinkle with cheese.

Touch of Green Soup
with Goat Cheese Topping

Makes about 6 servings

 A very special combination of flavors, designed to impress your guests.

1 medium head cauliflower, cut into flowerets
1 celery stalk, coarsely chopped
1 small leek, thinly sliced
3 cups chicken broth
½ teaspoon salt
⅛ teaspoon white pepper
¼ cup dry white wine
½ cup crumbled goat cheese (about 2½ oz.)
¼ cup toasted chopped pine nuts or pistachios (see Note, page 9)

Combine cauliflower, celery, leek, broth, salt, pepper and wine in a slow cooker. Cover and cook on LOW 9 to 10 hours or until vegetables are tender. Process in a blender or food processor until pureed. Reheat soup until hot if needed. Pour into individual soup bowls. Top with goat cheese and chopped nuts.

Hamburger Soup
Makes 5 or 6 servings

You can put together this hearty soup in the morning, then have it ready when everyone comes home for dinner.

1 lb. lean ground beef
¼ teaspoon pepper
¼ teaspoon dried oregano
¼ teaspoon dried basil
¼ teaspoon seasoned salt
1 (about 1-oz.) envelope dry onion soup mix
3 cups boiling water
1 (8-oz.) can tomato sauce
1 tablespoon soy sauce
1 cup sliced celery
1 cup thinly sliced carrots
1 cup macaroni, cooked and drained
¼ cup grated Parmesan cheese
2 tablespoons chopped fresh parsley

Crumble beef into a slow cooker. Add pepper, oregano, basil, seasoned salt and dry soup mix. Stir in water, tomato sauce, and soy sauce, then add celery and carrots. Cover and cook on LOW 6 to 8 hours. Turn control to HIGH. Add cooked macaroni and Parmesan cheese. Cover and cook on HIGH 10 to 15 minutes. Sprinkle with parsley just before serving. Serve hot.

Minestrone Soup

Makes 8 to 10 servings

This traditional dish is served in many Italian restaurants. Cannellini beans are white kidney beans and are usually only available in cans.

1 lb. beef stew meat, cut into 1-inch cubes
6 cups beef broth
1 onion, chopped
1 teaspoon dried thyme
2 tablespoons minced fresh parsley
½ teaspoon salt
¼ teaspoon pepper
1 (16-oz.) can peeled diced tomatoes in juice
2 cups chopped cabbage
1 (15-oz.) can cannellini beans, drained
1 zucchini, thinly sliced
1 cup uncooked small elbow macaroni (about 4½ oz.)
¼ cup grated Parmesan cheese

In a slow cooker, combine beef, broth, onion, thyme, parsley, salt, pepper, tomatoes and cabbage. Cover and cook on LOW 9 to 10 hours or until meat is tender. Turn control to HIGH. Add drained beans, zucchini and macaroni. Cover and cook on HIGH 30 to 45 minutes or until zucchini and macaroni are tender. Spoon hot soup into bowls. Top with cheese.

Oxtail Soup

Makes 6 to 8 servings

This richly flavored soup is a meal in itself. If leeks are not available, substitute one onion.

1 lb. oxtails
1 tomato, chopped
1 carrot, peeled and chopped
1 turnip, peeled and sliced
1 leek, halved and sliced
1 clove garlic, crushed
½ cup rosé wine
5 to 6 cups water
½ teaspoon dried dill weed
½ cup frozen green peas
1 tablespoon chopped fresh basil

Combine oxtails, tomato, carrot, turnip, leek, garlic, wine, water, dill and peas in a slow cooker. Cover and cook on LOW 4 to 6 hours. Remove oxtails; chop meat and discard bones. Return meat to cooker. Cover and cook on LOW 2 to 3 hours. Add peas about 30 minutes before serving. Sprinkle with basil and serve hot.

Georgia Peanut Soup

Makes 4 servings

Embellish each serving with about a tablespoon of chopped peanuts on the top, if desired.

3 cups chicken broth
¼ cup finely chopped celery
¼ teaspoon salt
1 small onion, finely chopped
2 tablespoons margarine or butter
½ cup peanut butter
1 cup milk or half-and-half
2 tablespoons cornstarch dissolved in ¼ cup water

Combine chicken stock, celery, salt, onion, margarine or butter, and peanut butter in a slow cooker. Cover and cook on HIGH 2 to 3 hours. Add milk or half-and-half and cornstarch mixture. Cover and cook on HIGH 15 to 20 minutes or until slightly thickened, stirring several times. Serve hot.

Sweet-Hot Pumpkin Soup

Makes 5 or 6 servings

Choose either one or two jalapeño chiles, depending on how "hot" you enjoy your soup.

1 (16-oz.) can pumpkin
4 cups chicken broth
2 carrots, peeled and chopped
1 onion, chopped
2 tablespoons chopped watercress
1 or 2 jalapeño chiles, seeded and chopped
3 tablespoons honey
½ teaspoon curry powder
½ teaspoon salt
¼ cup Sauterne wine
Watercress leaves for garnish

Combine pumpkin, chicken broth, carrots, onion, watercress, chiles, honey, curry powder, salt and wine in a slow cooker. Cover and cook on LOW 9 to 9½ hours or until vegetables are very soft. Process in a blender or food processor until pureed. Reheat soup until hot if needed. Garnish with additional watercress leaves.

Golden Squash Soup with Pesto Topping

Makes 6 to 8 servings

 This mild-flavored soup comes alive with flavor when topped with zesty pesto.

2 lbs. banana squash
1 onion, finely chopped
1 celery stalk with leaves, sliced crosswise
1 clove garlic, crushed
3 cups chicken broth or bouillon
½ teaspoon salt
⅛ teaspoon pepper
Jalapeño Pesto (see below)
½ cup light evaporated milk or half-and-half

JALAPEÑO PESTO
1 fresh jalapeño chile, seeded and finely chopped
¼ cup coarsely chopped cilantro leaves
1 small yellow or red bell pepper, chopped
2 tablespoons sun-dried tomatoes in oil, drained and chopped
2 tablespoons olive oil

Peel squash; cut into 1-inch cubes. In a slow cooker, combine squash, onion, celery, garlic, broth, salt and pepper. Cover and cook on LOW 7 to 8 hours or until vegetables are soft. While soup is cooking prepare pesto.

Process soup in a blender or food processor until pureed. Return to the slow cooker or to a saucepan. Add evaporated milk or half-and-half and heat to desired temperature. Pour into individual soup bowls. Top each serving with 1½ to 2 tablespoons pesto.

Jalapeño Pesto

In a small bowl, combine chopped jalapeño, cilantro, bell pepper, sun-dried tomatoes and olive oil.

Hearty Alphabet Soup
Makes 6 or 7 servings

 Did you ever have fun trying to spell your name with the noodles in the soup?

½ lb. beef stew meat or round steak
1 (1-lb.) can Italian-style diced tomatoes
1 (8-oz.) can tomato sauce
3 cups water
1 (about 1-oz.) envelope onion soup mix
½ cup uncooked alphabet noodles
1 (16-oz.) package frozen Italian-style vegetables, cooked

Cut beef into small cubes. In a slow cooker, combine meat, tomatoes, tomato sauce, water and dry soup mix. Cover and cook on LOW 6 to 8 hours or until meat is tender. Turn control to HIGH. Add noodles. Cover and cook on HIGH 15 to 20 minutes or until noodles are cooked. Stir in cooked, drained vegetables. Serve hot.

Split-Pea Soup

Makes 8 servings

 This style of pea soup is also known as "Dutch" pea soup.

1 (1-lb.) package split peas
1 ham bone (with some meat left on) or 2 ham hocks
1 carrot, peeled and diced
1 onion, diced
1 small potato, peeled and diced
1 small smoked sausage, sliced
1 celery stalk, diced
8 cups water
½ teaspoon salt
¼ teaspoon pepper

Combine peas, ham bone or hocks, carrot, onion, potato, sausage, celery, water, salt and pepper in a slow cooker. Cover and cook on LOW 8 to 10 hours. Remove ham bone; cut meat off bones, dice meat, and discard bones. Return meat to soup. Serve soup hot.

Swedish Cabbage Soup

Makes 8 servings

Lamb creates a very rich-flavored broth that is the perfect match for these winter vegetables.

1 lamb shank
1 beef bouillon cube
¼ teaspoon pepper
¼ teaspoon salt
1½ teaspoons whole allspice
1 leek, chopped
1 parsnip, peeled and diced
1 carrot, peeled and diced
¼ cup thinly sliced celery
1 medium potato, peeled and diced
2 tablespoons minced fresh parsley
4 cups water
4 cups shredded cabbage

Place lamb shank in a slow cooker with bouillon cube, pepper, and salt. Tie allspice in a cheesecloth bag. Add allspice, leek, parsnip, carrot, celery, potato, parsley and water to cooker. Cover and cook on LOW 7 to 9 hours or until meat is tender. Remove allspice and meat from cooker. Cut meat off bones, dice meat, and discard bones. Return meat to cooker. Skim off fat from top of soup. Turn control to HIGH. Add cabbage. Cover and cook on HIGH 25 to 30 minutes or until cabbage is done. Spoon hot soup into bowls.

French Onion Soup

Makes 4 servings

 Serve with a sandwich for an easy supper.

3 large onions, thinly sliced
¼ cup margarine or butter
4 cups beef broth
1 teaspoon Worcestershire sauce
¼ teaspoon salt
4 to 5 slices French bread, toasted
¼ cup grated Parmesan cheese

In a slow cooker, combine onions and margarine or butter, broth, Worcestershire sauce and salt. Cover and cook on HIGH 4 to 6 hours. Pour hot soup into individual bowls. Top each bowl with toasted French bread and sprinkle with cheese.

Herbed Spinach Soup
Makes 8 servings

 You don't have to be Popeye to appreciate this soup. Serve it with hot biscuits.

3 green onions, finely chopped
3 parsley sprigs
¼ small head lettuce, sliced
1 bunch fresh spinach
2 tablespoons margarine or butter
½ teaspoon salt
⅛ teaspoon pepper
1 teaspoon dried tarragon
4 (10½-oz.) cans condensed beef broth
½ cup half-and-half
1 hard-cooked egg, chopped
Pinch freshly grated nutmeg

In a slow cooker, combine onions, parsley, lettuce, spinach, margarine or butter, salt, pepper, tarragon and broth. Cover and cook on LOW 4 to 6 hours. Process in a blender or food processor in batches until vegetables are finely chopped. Turn control to HIGH. Pour blended mixture into the slow cooker. Stir in half-and-half. Cover and cook on HIGH 20 to 30 minutes. Serve hot, garnished with chopped hard-cooked egg and a pinch of nutmeg.

Tavern Soup

Makes 6 to 8 servings

 Years ago, a tavern was the place to go for a good home-cooked meal.

1 celery stalk, thinly sliced
1 carrot, peeled and thinly sliced
¼ cup finely chopped green bell pepper
1 small onion, finely chopped
3 (14½-oz.) cans chicken broth
1 (12-oz.) can light beer, room temperature
½ teaspoon salt
¼ teaspoon pepper
5 tablespoons cornstarch
¼ cup water
1 cup (4 oz.) shredded sharp Cheddar cheese

Combine celery, carrot, bell pepper and onion in a slow cooker. Add broth, beer, salt and pepper. Cover and cook on LOW 5 to 6 hours. Process vegetables in a blender or food processor in batches until pureed and return to cooker with broth. Turn control to HIGH. Dissolve cornstarch in water; stir into pureed mixture. Add cheese gradually, stirring until blended. Cover and cook on HIGH 15 to 20 minutes. Serve hot.

Tortilla Soup

Makes 5 or 6 servings

 Topped with thin strips of tortillas, this soup has a slightly spicy flavor.

2 chicken breast halves, boned, skinned and cubed
1 onion, finely chopped
1 clove garlic, crushed
3 medium tomatoes, peeled, seeded and chopped
4 cups chicken broth
¼ teaspoon salt
⅛ teaspoon pepper
1 mild green chile, seeded and chopped
2 tablespoons vegetable oil
4 corn tortillas, halved and cut into ¼-inch strips
2 tablespoons coarsely chopped fresh cilantro

Combine chicken, onion, garlic, tomatoes, broth, salt, pepper and green chile in a slow cooker. Cover and cook on LOW 7 to 8 hours. Process in a food processor or blender until pureed. Heat oil in a large skillet. Add tortilla strips. Cook, stirring, over medium heat until crisp; drain on paper towels. Reheat soup if needed and spoon into individual bowls. Top with crisp tortilla strips. Sprinkle with cilantro.

Turkey Noodle Soup
Makes 8 servings

 This is the perfect soup to make from your leftover Thanksgiving turkey.

1 turkey carcass, broken into several pieces
2 quarts water
1 teaspoon salt
¼ teaspoon pepper
1 onion, chopped
2 celery stalks, chopped
1 carrot, peeled and chopped
2 tablespoons chopped fresh parsley
½ teaspoon dried marjoram
1 bay leaf
6 oz. noodles, cooked and drained

Combine turkey carcass and water in a slow cooker. Add salt, pepper, onion, celery, carrot, parsley, marjoram and bay leaf. Cover and cook on LOW 5 to 6 hours. Remove carcass and bay leaf from cooker. Take meat off bones; return meat to broth. Discard bones. Add cooked noodles to cooker. Cover and cook on HIGH 20 to 30 minutes. Discard bay leaf. Serve soup hot.

VARIATION: This recipe is designed for a 4½-quart slow cooker. For a 3½-quart or smaller slow cooker, use chunks of turkey meat cut off the bones, or chicken parts.

Congressional Bean Soup

Makes 6 to 8 servings

Here is my version of the famous bean soup prepared regularly for the U.S. Senate.

8 cups water
1 lb. dried small white beans
1 meaty ham bone or 2 cups diced cooked ham
1 cup finely chopped celery
1 onion, finely chopped
2 tablespoons finely chopped fresh parsley
1 teaspoon salt
¼ teaspoon pepper
1 bay leaf

In a large pan, bring water to a boil. Add beans and boil gently 2 minutes. Turn off heat and let stand 1 hour. Pour into a slow cooker. Add remaining ingredients. Cover and cook on LOW 12 to 14 hours or until beans are very soft. Remove bay leaf and ham bone. Cut meat off bone; return meat to beans. Discard bone and bay leaf. Serve soup hot.

VARIATION: The beans may be soaked overnight in the water if preferred.

Killarney Chowder

Makes 4 to 6 servings

A sprinkle of watercress tops off this soup with an Irish accent. Serve this wonderful dish on Saint Patrick's Day.

2 leeks
3 small potatoes, peeled and chopped
3½ cups chicken stock
1 (10-oz.) package frozen green peas, thawed
½ cup coarsely chopped watercress leaves
½ teaspoon seasoned salt
⅛ teaspoon pepper
½ cup sour cream
Watercress leaves

Trim and clean leeks; slice crosswise. In a slow cooker, combine leeks. potatoes, stock, peas, watercress, seasoned salt, and pepper. Cover and cook on LOW 5 to 6 hours or until vegetables are tender. Process one-third of the mixture at a time in a blender or food processor until pureed. Return mixture to cooker. Turn control to HIGH. Stir in sour cream. Cook on HIGH 15 to 20 minutes or until hot. Spoon into bowls. Garnish with a few watercress leaves.

Down East Corn Chowder
Makes 6 to 8 servings

 Your friends will enjoy the wholesome flavor of this simple chowder.

3 cups fresh corn kernels, cut from cob, or 2 (16-oz.) cans whole-kernel corn,
    drained
2 medium potatoes, peeled and finely chopped
1 onion, finely chopped
½ teaspoon seasoned salt
⅛ teaspoon pepper
2 cups chicken broth
2 cups milk
¼ cup margarine or butter
Ground mace

Combine corn, potatoes, onion, seasoned salt, pepper and broth in a slow cooker. Cover and cook on LOW 7 to 9 hours. Pour into a blender or food processor and puree until almost smooth. Cover and refrigerate overnight, if desired, or return to cooker. Stir in milk and margarine or butter. Cover and cook on HIGH 1 hour. Pour hot soup into bowls; sprinkle with mace.

New England Clam Chowder

Makes 6 or 7 servings

There are two types of clam chowder: New England always contains milk or cream; Manhattan has tomatoes instead of the milk.

2 oz. salt pork or bacon, cut in small cubes
1 onion, chopped
2 medium potatoes, peeled and diced
½ teaspoon salt
⅛ teaspoon pepper
1 (8-oz.) bottle clam juice
2 cups water
2 (7-oz.) cans minced clams, drained, or 1 pint shucked fresh clams, cut up
2 cups half-and-half or evaporated milk
Paprika

Cook salt pork with onion in a skillet over medium heat until onion is softened. Combine pork and onion with potatoes, salt, pepper, clam juice and water in a slow cooker. Cover and cook on LOW 5 to 7 hours. Turn control to HIGH. Add clams and half-and-half. Cover and cook on HIGH 15 minutes. Serve hot, sprinkled with paprika.

Bouillabaisse

Makes 6 or 7 servings

Dip slices of bread into this version of the French classic, which contains mixed seafood and a flavorful broth.

1 carrot, peeled and chopped
1 onion, chopped
1 clove garlic, minced
1 (1-lb.) can tomatoes, cut up
3 cups water
2 bay leaves
2 cups beef broth
¼ cup chopped fresh parsley
½ teaspoon dried thyme, crushed
1 tablespoon salt
1 teaspoon fresh lemon juice
A pinch powdered saffron or 1 teaspoon turmeric
¼ lb. large uncooked shrimp, shelled
½ lb. fresh or frozen fish fillets, thawed and cut into 2-inch chunks
1 uncooked lobster tail, cut into 2-inch chunks
French bread

In a 4-quart or larger slow cooker, combine carrot, onion, garlic, tomatoes, water, bay leaves, broth, parsley, thyme, salt, lemon juice, and saffron or turmeric. Cover and cook on LOW 6 to 8 hours. Strain; return broth to cooker. Turn control to HIGH. Add shrimp, fish fillets, and lobster. Cover cooker and cook on HIGH 20 to 30 minutes or until seafood is done. Serve hot in large bowls with French bread.

VARIATION: If using cooked lobster tails, add them 5 minutes before serving.

Barbecue Beef Sandwiches

Makes 4 or 5 servings

Leftover meat takes on a new role as a filling for a hot sandwich. Serve over warm cornbread for a real treat.

2 cups thinly sliced cooked beef or pork
2 tablespoons instant minced onion
1 tablespoon brown sugar
1 teaspoon paprika
½ teaspoon dried oregano, crushed
1 teaspoon chili powder
½ teaspoon cracked pepper
¼ teaspoon salt
1 bay leaf
1 clove garlic, minced
1 cup ketchup
¼ cup water
1 tablespoon salad oil
¼ cup tarragon vinegar
2 tablespoons Worcestershire sauce
2 or 3 drops liquid smoke

Combine all ingredients in a slow cooker. Cover and cook on LOW 4 to 6 hours. Remove and discard bay leaf. Serve hot over French rolls or toast.

Chili Dogs
Makes 8 to 10 servings

 For a larger group, double the recipe and keep hot in the slow cooker; let guests serve themselves.

1 (15-oz.) can chili with beans	1 teaspoon prepared mustard
1 (6-oz.) can tomato paste	½ teaspoon salt
¼ cup minced green bell pepper	½ teaspoon chili powder
¼ cup minced onion	8 to 10 hot dogs and hot dog buns

In a slow cooker, combine chili with beans, tomato paste, bell pepper, onion, mustard, salt and chili powder. Cover and cook on LOW 3 to 4 hours. In a large saucepan, cook hot dogs in boiling water, or microwave. Toast buns. Serve a hot dog on each bun. Spoon chili mixture over hot dogs.

Sloppy Jane Sandwiches
Makes 5 or 6 servings

These are a special favorite of the younger generation.

1 package (about 10) hot dogs, sliced	1 teaspoon instant minced onion
1 (28-oz.) can baked beans	⅓ cup chili sauce
1 teaspoon prepared mustard	5 to 6 hot dog buns, toasted

In a slow cooker, combine hot dogs, beans, mustard, onion, and chili sauce. Cover and cook on LOW 2 to 3 hours. Spoon over toasted hot dog buns.

Sloppy Joes

Makes 6 or 7 servings

A great way to feed a hungry group of people. Let friends spoon up their own servings. A popular dish for teenagers.

1½ lbs. extra-lean ground beef
1 small onion, minced
2 celery stalks, minced
1 (12-oz.) bottle chili sauce
1 tablespoon brown sugar
1 tablespoon Worcestershire sauce
½ teaspoon salt
2 tablespoons sweet pickle relish
⅛ teaspoon pepper
Hamburger buns or French rolls, toasted

In a slow cooker, combine meat, onion, celery, chili sauce, brown sugar, Worcestershire sauce, salt, relish and pepper. Cover and cook on LOW 3 to 4 hours. If possible, break up meat with a fork or spoon once during cooking, then re-cover to continue cooking. Spoon over toasted hamburger buns or French rolls.

VARIATION: Recipe may be doubled and mixture kept warm in slow cooker for an after-the-game party.

Ham-Stuffed French Rolls

Makes 6 to 8 servings

 Foil wrapping keeps these piping hot until you're ready to serve.

2 cups finely chopped cooked ham
2 hard-cooked eggs, finely chopped
2 tablespoons minced green onion
2 tablespoons chopped ripe olives (optional)
1 teaspoon prepared mustard
1 teaspoon sweet pickle relish
½ cup small cubes Cheddar cheese
⅓ cup mayonnaise
6 large or 8 small French rolls
Foil squares

In a large bowl, combine ham, eggs, onion, olives, mustard, relish, cheese and mayonnaise. Cut off tops or one end of rolls; scoop out most of soft center. Fill with ham mixture. Replace top or end of roll. Wrap each roll in foil. Place filled rolls in a slow cooker. Cover and heat on LOW 2 to 3 hours. Rolls may be kept hot and served from the cooker.

Welsh Rarebit
Makes 4 to 6 servings

In some parts of the country this is known as Welsh Rabbit. Whichever name you use, you know it means good eating.

1 (12-oz.) can beer
1 tablespoon dry mustard
1 teaspoon Worcestershire sauce
½ teaspoon salt
⅛ teaspoon pepper
1 lb. processed American cheese, cut into cubes
1 lb. sharp Cheddar cheese, cut into cubes
Bread slices or English muffins, toasted
Cooked bacon strips
Tomato slices

In a slow cooker, combine beer, mustard, Worcestershire sauce, salt and pepper. Cover and cook on HIGH 1 to 2 hours or until mixture boils. Add cheese a little at a time, stirring constantly, until all the cheese has melted. Heat on HIGH 20 to 30 minutes with lid off, stirring frequently. Serve hot over toasted bread or English muffins. Garnish with strips of crisp bacon and tomato slices.

Beef

 Slow cooking makes beef so tender it nearly melts in your mouth! You'll love the rich and succulent flavors provided by simmering beef in the slow cooker.

You can enjoy a variety of internationally inspired recipes, including Slow-Cooker Fajitas and Swedish Cabbage Rolls. Creole-Asian Strips combines two distinct cuisines in a delightfully different mix of spices. Try newly available ingredients like dried shiitake mushrooms, featured in Black Forest Pot Roast.

Included are the best traditional favorites as well as new recipes. Beef provides main dishes for family meals and entertaining. By planning ahead, you can cook a dish now, freeze it, and serve it as a quick meal when needed. Try Flank Steak in Mushroom Wine Sauce for entertaining. Or, consider Beef Burgundy or California Tamale Pie for an especially satisfying family dinner.

It is not necessary to brown meat before you cook. Ordinarily, you can place most beef cuts directly in the bottom of the slow cooker with the seasonings and vegetables. When meat is fatty or when you don't want it to cook in the juices, put it on a rack, trivet or steamer basket placed on the bottom of the cooker. You can also create a vegetable rack by placing carrots, onions or potatoes in the cooker first, and then placing the meat on top of them.

You will notice a range of cooking times for all of the beef recipes. That's another advantage of slow cookers—you can leave in the morning, let the meat cook most of the day, and not worry about it sticking, burning or overcooking should you return later than expected. The low temperature is so low that an hour or two makes very little difference in slow-cooking recipes.

How do you decide when the beef is done? Cook until the minimum time suggested for the recipe. Then, just test it with a fork to see if it is as tender as you prefer. The thickness of the cut of beef, distribution of fat and amount of bone will change the cooking time, so always check before assuming the meat is ready to serve.

Here is a secret for cooking vegetables with beef: Some vegetables take as long or longer to cook than beef. If you plan a beef dish with large chunks of carrots or celery, place these in the bottom or around the sides of the pot and cover them with liquid such as water, broth or tomato sauce. You may want to cut them slightly smaller than usual. Slow cookers are notoriously slow for cooking vegetables, and smaller pieces cook faster.

Another secret: The good juices of meat don't evaporate. As a result, you have more liquid with a rich, meaty flavor. In most cases you can stir in dissolved cornstarch or flour after the meat is done. Then cook on high for a few minutes to thicken the gravy. Sauce and gravy lovers will enjoy Spicy Brisket over Noodles or Scandinavian Dilled Pot Roast.

Black Forest Pot Roast

Makes 6 or 7 servings

Dried shiitakes are often labeled Black Forest mushrooms; they may be found in the produce section or in the Oriental food section of your market.

1 (3- to 3½-lb.) boneless beef chuck or round bone roast
1 onion, chopped
¼ cup water
4 dried shiitake mushrooms, stems removed, crumbled, and rinsed
¼ cup ketchup
¼ cup dry red wine
2 tablespoons Dijon-style mustard
1 tablespoon Worcestershire sauce
½ teaspoon salt
⅛ teaspoon pepper
1 clove garlic, crushed
2 tablespoons cornstarch
3 tablespoons water

Trim all visible fat from meat; place in a slow cooker. In a small bowl, combine onion, water, mushrooms, ketchup, wine, mustard, Worcestershire sauce, salt, pepper and garlic. Pour mixture over meat. Cover and cook on LOW about 8 hours. Remove meat and slice. Keep meat warm. Turn control to HIGH. Dissolve cornstarch in water; stir into cooker. Cover and cook on HIGH 15 to 20 minutes or until thickened. Serve sauce with meat.

Beef Burritos

Makes 6 to 8 servings

Shredded cheese and your favorite salsa may be added to this traditional combination.

2 lbs. boneless beef chuck or other pot roast
1 jalapeño chile, seeded and finely chopped
1 garlic clove, crushed
1 teaspoon beef bouillon granules or 1 beef bouillon cube
1 onion, chopped
½ teaspoon chili powder
½ teaspoon ground cumin
2 tablespoons chopped fresh cilantro
½ teaspoon salt
1 (16-oz.) can refried beans, heated
6 to 8 (12-inch) flour tortillas, warmed

Trim fat from beef and discard. In a slow cooker, combine meat, chile, garlic, bouillon granules or cube, onion, chili powder, cumin, cilantro and salt. Cover and cook on LOW 8 hours or until meat is very tender. Remove meat from slow cooker. With 2 forks, shred meat; combine with ¾ cup cooking juices. Spread warm tortillas with refried beans. Add shredded beef. Fold over tortilla sides, then roll up. Serve warm.

Favorite Pot Roast

Makes 6 or 7 servings

All the good traditional ingredients and flavors that we associate with pot roast are here.

1 (3- to 3½-lb.) beef rump or chuck roast
½ teaspoon salt
½ teaspoon seasoned salt
¼ teaspoon seasoned pepper
¼ teaspoon paprika
1 onion, cut into 8 wedges
3 carrots, peeled and cut into 1-inch slices
4 potatoes, cut into eighths
1 celery stalk, coarsely chopped
1 cup beef broth
3 tablespoons cornstarch
¼ cup water

Trim visible fat from meat. Rub all sides of meat with salt, seasoned salt, seasoned pepper and paprika. Place vegetables in bottom of a slow cooker. Pour broth over vegetables. Place seasoned meat on top of vegetables. Cover and cook on LOW 8 to 9 hours or until meat and vegetables are tender. To thicken juices, remove meat and vegetables; keep warm. Turn control to HIGH. Dissolve cornstarch in water; stir into cooker. Cover and cook on HIGH 15 to 20 minutes or until slightly thickened. Serve with meat and vegetables.

Flemish Carbonades

Makes 5 to 7 servings

 Beer acts as a tenderizer and adds its own unique flavor.

2 to 3 lbs. boneless beef chuck, cut into 1-inch cubes
1 onion, thinly sliced
1 teaspoon salt
⅛ teaspoon pepper
2 teaspoons brown sugar
1 clove garlic, minced
1 (12-oz.) can beer
2 bacon slices, cooked and crumbled
3 tablespoons cornstarch
¼ cup water
Cooked noodles

In a slow cooker, combine meat, onion, salt, pepper, brown sugar, garlic, beer and bacon. Cover and cook on LOW 5 to 7 hours or until meat is tender. Turn control to HIGH. Dissolve cornstarch in water. Stir into meat mixture. Cover and cook on HIGH 20 to 30 minutes or until slightly thickened. Serve over noodles.

Old World Sauerbraten

Makes 8 servings

 A traditional main dish with enticing flavors and aromas.

1 (3½- to 4-lb.) beef rump or sirloin tip roast
1 cup water
1 cup vinegar
1 large onion, sliced
1 lemon (unpeeled), sliced
1 tablespoon salt
2 tablespoons sugar
10 whole cloves
4 bay leaves
6 whole peppercorns
12 gingersnaps, crumbled

Place meat in a deep ceramic or glass bowl. Combine water, vinegar, onion, lemon, salt and sugar. Tie cloves, bay leaves, and peppercorns in a cheesecloth bag. Add to bowl. Pour marinade over meat. Cover and refrigerate 24 to 36 hours; turn meat several times during marinating.

Place beef in a slow cooker. Pour 1 cup of the marinade over meat, cover, and cook on LOW 6 to 8 hours. Place meat on a serving platter and keep warm. Strain meat juices and return to cooker. Turn control to HIGH. Remove cheesecloth bag. Stir in gingersnaps, cover, and cook on HIGH 15 to 20 minutes. Slice meat and serve with sauce.

Pot Roast with Creamy Mushroom Sauce
Makes 6 to 8 servings

Each package of dry onion soup mix contains two envelopes; use one envelope for this pot roast.

1 (2- to 2½-lb.) boneless beef chuck roast
1 (about 1-oz.) envelope dry onion soup mix
1 (10¾-oz.) can condensed cream of mushroom soup
Mashed potatoes or cooked noodles

Place roast in a slow cooker. Add dry onion soup mix; top with undiluted mushroom soup. Cover and cook on LOW 6 to 8 hours or until meat is tender. Slice and serve with mashed potatoes or over cooked noodles.

Scandinavian Dilled Pot Roast

Makes 6 to 8 servings

This hearty main dish is considered a symbol of hospitality in Scandinavia. If desired, place two or three baking potatoes on top of the roast and remove before making gravy.

1 (3- to 3½-lb.) beef rump or chuck roast
½ teaspoon salt
¼ teaspoon pepper
2 teaspoons dried dill weed
¼ cup water
1 tablespoon vinegar
4 teaspoons cornstarch
2 tablespoons water
1 cup sour cream

Sprinkle all sides of meat with salt, pepper, and 1 teaspoon of the dill. Place in a slow cooker. Add water and vinegar. Cover and cook on LOW 7 to 9 hours or until tender. Place meat on a platter and keep warm. Turn control to HIGH. Dissolve cornstarch in water; stir into meat drippings. Stir in remaining 1 teaspoon dill. Cook on HIGH about 10 to 15 minutes or until slightly thickened. Stir in sour cream. Slice meat; serve with sauce.

Slow-Cooker Fajitas

Makes 8 to 10 servings

Strips of beef or chicken absorb the flavors of the sauce during the slow-cooking process.

1½ to 2 lbs. flank or skirt steak, or boneless chicken
1 onion, thinly sliced
1 red or green bell pepper, sliced
1 clove garlic, crushed
1 jalapeño chile, seeded and finely chopped
2 teaspoons chili powder
½ teaspoon ground cumin
¼ teaspoon salt
¼ cup vegetable oil
1 tablespoon fresh lemon juice
8 to 10 warm flour tortillas
½ cup sour cream
1 avocado, peeled, pitted and thinly sliced

Cut meat across the grain into ½-inch diagonal strips. Place in a slow cooker. Top with onion and bell pepper. In a small bowl, combine garlic, chile, chili powder, cumin, salt, oil and lemon juice. Pour mixture over meat. Cover and cook on LOW 6 to 7 hours or until meat is tender. Spoon several slices of meat with sauce into center of each warm tortilla. Fold over. Top with sour cream and avocado.

Glazed Corned Beef

Makes 6 to 8 servings

 Zesty seasonings create an appetizing finishing touch to cooked corned beef.

1 (3½- to 4-lb.) corned beef brisket
2 tablespoons prepared mustard
1½ teaspoons cream-style horseradish
2 tablespoons red wine vinegar
¼ cup molasses

In a slow cooker, cover corned beef with water. Cover and cook on LOW 10 to 12 hours or until tender. Drain corned beef; place on a broiler pan or ovenproof platter. Preheat oven to 400F (205C). In a small bowl, combine mustard, horseradish, vinegar and molasses. Brush on all sides of meat. Bake, brushing with sauce several times, about 20 minutes or until meat begins to brown. Cut into thin slices.

Corned Beef

Makes 6 to 8 servings

 Choose your favorite mustard to accompany this dish: Dijon, coarse-grain or just plain old-fashioned yellow. Tender steamed cabbage is a traditional side dish.

1 (2½- to 3-lb.) corned beef brisket with pickling spices
1 medium onion, chopped
1 carrot, peeled and coarsely shredded
1 clove garlic, minced or pureed

Place corned beef in a slow cooker. Top with pickling spices, onion, carrot and garlic. Add enough water to cover meat. Cover and cook on LOW 8 to 9 hours or until meat is tender. Remove from cooker; slice and serve.

Spicy Brisket over Noodles

Makes 5 or 6 servings

The intensity of "heat" varies with different picante sauces; choose the one that suits your taste.

1 (2- to 2½-lb.) lean beef brisket
½ teaspoon salt
¼ teaspoon pepper
1 onion, sliced
1 celery stalk, chopped
1 cup picante sauce
1 (12-oz.) can beer
2 tablespoons cornstarch
3 tablespoons water
Cooked noodles

Trim visible fat from brisket. Combine beef, salt, pepper, onion, celery, picante sauce and beer in a slow cooker. Cover and cook on LOW 7 to 9 hours or until meat is tender. Remove meat and vegetables from cooker. Skim off any excess fat. Turn control to HIGH. Dissolve cornstarch in water. Gradually add to liquid in cooker, stirring constantly. Cover and cook on HIGH, stirring every 10 minutes, about 20 minutes or until thickened. Cut meat into diagonal slices; arrange on noodles. Top with thickened sauce.

California Tamale Pie
Makes 6 to 8 servings

Here is the ideal dish for serving on the patio or porch. Serve it directly from the cooker.

¾ cup yellow cornmeal
1 cup milk
1 egg, slightly beaten
1 lb. extra-lean ground beef
1 teaspoon chili powder
½ teaspoon ground cumin
1 teaspoon seasoned salt
1 (14- to 15-oz.) can chunky tomato salsa
1 (16-oz.) can whole-kernel corn, drained
1 (2.25-oz. drained weight) can sliced ripe olives, drained
1 cup (4 oz.) shredded Cheddar cheese

In a large bowl, mix cornmeal, milk and egg. Stir in meat, chili powder, cumin, salt, salsa, corn and olives. Pour mixture into a slow cooker. Cover and cook on HIGH 3 to 4 hours. Sprinkle cheese over top; cover and cook another 5 minutes.

Cheddar Cheese Meat Loaf

Makes 6 or 7 servings

Cheesecloth helps to hold meat together while lifting it into and out of the cooker.

¾ cup crushed cheese crackers
1 small onion, finely chopped
2 tablespoons minced green bell pepper
¼ cup chili sauce
½ cup milk
2 eggs, beaten slightly
½ teaspoon salt
⅛ teaspoon pepper
1½ lbs. lean ground beef
1 cup (4 oz.) shredded Cheddar cheese

In a large bowl, combine cracker crumbs, onion, bell pepper, chili sauce, milk, eggs, salt, pepper, ground beef and cheese. Form into a 6- or 7-inch round loaf. Place loaf on a 24 × 9-inch piece of cheesecloth. Place rack in a slow cooker. Gently lift loaf into cooker and place on rack. Loosely fold cheesecloth over top of meat. Cover and cook on LOW about 5 hours or until done. Holding ends of cheesecloth, lift cooked loaf from cooker. Remove cheesecloth; cut meat into 6 or 7 wedges.

Family Favorite Meat Loaf

Makes 6 servings

 This is a time-honored dish that cooks while you're at work or play.

2 eggs, beaten
¾ cup milk
⅔ cup fine dry bread crumbs
2 tablespoons grated onion
½ teaspoon salt
½ teaspoon ground sage
1½ lbs. lean ground beef
¼ cup ketchup
2 tablespoons brown sugar
1 teaspoon dry mustard
¼ teaspoon freshly grated nutmeg

In a large bowl, combine eggs, milk, bread crumbs, onion, salt, sage and meat. Mix well and shape into a 9 × 5-inch rectangle or oval, or about a 6-inch round. Carefully place in a slow cooker. Cover and cook on LOW 5 to 6 hours. Combine ketchup, brown sugar, mustard and nutmeg in a small bowl; pour mixture over meat. Turn control to HIGH. Cover and cook on HIGH 15 minutes. Slice and serve while hot or use cold slices for sandwiches.

Italian Meatball Stew

Makes 5 or 6 servings

You can vary this dish with your favorite combination of frozen or fresh vegetables.

1½ lbs. extra-lean ground beef
½ cup fine dry bread crumbs
2 eggs, slightly beaten
¼ cup milk
2 tablespoons grated Parmesan cheese
½ teaspoon salt
¼ teaspoon pepper
1 clove garlic, crushed
1 (6-oz.) can tomato paste
2 cups beef broth
½ teaspoon seasoned salt
½ teaspoon dried oregano, crushed
½ teaspoon dried basil, crushed
1 (16-oz.) package frozen Italian-style vegetables, cooked and drained

In a large bowl, combine beef with bread crumbs, eggs, milk, cheese, salt, pepper and garlic. Form into 2-inch balls. Place meatballs in bottom of slow cooker. Combine tomato paste, broth, seasoned salt, oregano and basil. Pour mixture over meat. Cover and cook on LOW 4½ to 5 hours. Stir in cooked vegetables. Cover and cook on HIGH 10 to 15 minutes or until mixture is hot.

Shell Casserole

Makes 4 or 5 servings

The children in our family request this over and over; see if yours like it as well.

1 lb. lean ground beef
1 small onion, chopped
½ teaspoon salt
¼ teaspoon garlic powder
1 teaspoon Worcestershire sauce
¼ cup all-purpose flour
1¼ cups hot water
2 teaspoons beef bouillon granules
2 tablespoons red wine
6 oz. large shell-shaped pasta
1 (2-oz.) can sliced mushrooms, drained
1 cup sour cream

In a skillet, cook ground beef and onion until red color disappears. Drain beef; place in a slow cooker. Stir in salt, garlic powder, Worcestershire sauce and flour. Add water, bouillon and wine; mix well. Cover and cook on LOW 2 to 3 hours. Meanwhile, cook pasta according to package directions and drain. Add cooked pasta, mushrooms and sour cream to slow cooker; stir to mix ingredients. Turn control to HIGH. Cover and cook on HIGH 10 to 15 minutes.

Spaghetti Meat Sauce

Makes 6 to 8 servings

 Make the sauce ahead of time and freeze it; thaw and heat just before serving.

1 lb. lean ground beef
1 large onion, chopped
1 clove garlic, minced
2 (1-lb.) cans tomatoes, chopped
1 (8-oz.) can tomato sauce
1 (12-oz.) can tomato paste
1 cup beef broth
2 tablespoons minced fresh parsley
1 tablespoon brown sugar
1 teaspoon dried oregano leaves
1 teaspoon dried basil leaves
1 teaspoon salt
¼ teaspoon pepper
Cooked spaghetti, noodles, or other pasta

Break up pieces of meat with a fork. Combine meat in a slow cooker with re-maining ingredients. Cover and cook on LOW 6 to 8 hours. Serve over hot spaghetti, noodles, or other pasta.

Swedish Cabbage Rolls
Makes 12 rolls

 A handy dish to take to a potluck supper. Any leftovers freeze beautifully.

12 large cabbage leaves
1 egg, slightly beaten
¼ cup milk
¼ cup finely chopped onion
1 teaspoon salt
¼ teaspoon pepper
1 lb. lean ground beef
⅓ cup uncooked rice
1 (8-oz.) can tomato sauce
1 tablespoon brown sugar
1 tablespoon fresh lemon juice
1 teaspoon Worcestershire sauce

Immerse cabbage leaves in a large pot of boiling water and cook about 3 minutes or until limp; drain. In a large bowl, combine egg, milk, onion, salt, pepper, beef and rice. Place about 3 tablespoons of meat mixture in center of each cabbage leaf. Fold in sides and roll ends over meat mixture. Place in a slow cooker. In a small bowl, combine tomato sauce, brown sugar, lemon juice and Worcestershire sauce. Pour sauce over cabbage rolls. Cover and cook on LOW 6 to 7 hours. Serve hot, topped with sauce.

German Short Ribs

Makes 5 or 6 servings

Succulent ribs with a tangy sauce. Select short ribs with the minimum amount of fat.

3 to 3½ lbs. beef short ribs
½ teaspoon salt
⅛ teaspoon pepper
2 medium onions, thinly sliced
½ cup dry red wine
½ cup chili sauce
3 tablespoons brown sugar
3 tablespoons vinegar
1 tablespoon Worcestershire sauce
½ teaspoon dry mustard
½ teaspoon chili powder
2 tablespoons cornstarch
¼ cup water
Cooked noodles

In a slow cooker, combine ribs, salt, pepper, onions, wine, chili sauce, brown sugar, vinegar, Worcestershire sauce, mustard and chili powder. Cover and cook on LOW 6 to 8 hours. Turn control to HIGH. Dissolve cornstarch in water. Stir cornstarch mixture into rib mixture. Cover and cook on HIGH 10 to 15 minutes or until slightly thickened. Serve hot over cooked wide noodles.

Homestyle Short Ribs
Makes 4 to 6 servings

Here is an inexpensive cut of meat that becomes a satisfying meal. The hint of sweet and sour in the sauce gives added pleasure.

2½ to 3 lbs. lean beef short ribs
1 lb. red-skinned new potatoes, quartered
12 baby carrots, peeled and halved
1 onion, sliced
2 tablespoons cider or wine vinegar
2 tablespoons sugar
1 tablespoon cream-style horseradish
1 tablespoon prepared mustard
2 tablespoons ketchup
½ cup beef broth
¼ cup all-purpose flour
¼ cup water
Salt and pepper to taste

Preheat broiler. Place ribs on broiler rack and brown under broiler on both sides. Discard drippings. Place potatoes, carrots and onion in a slow cooker. Arrange browned ribs over vegetables. In a small bowl, combine vinegar, sugar, horseradish, mustard, ketchup and beef broth. Pour mixture over meat. Cover and cook on LOW 7 to 8 hours. Remove ribs and vegetables, cover, and keep warm. Turn control to HIGH. Combine flour and water; stir into sauce. Cover and cook on HIGH 15 to 20 minutes or until slightly thickened. Season with salt and pepper. Serve hot.

Marco Polo Short Ribs

Makes 4 to 6 servings

An appetizing discovery for short rib fans who enjoy a sauce that's not too highly spiced.

4 lbs. lean beef short ribs
1 large tomato, chopped
1 cup beef broth
¼ cup red wine
1 small onion, sliced
2 tablespoons prepared horseradish
1 teaspoon salt
¼ teaspoon pepper
½ teaspoon ground ginger
3 tablespoons cornstarch
3 tablespoons water

In a slow cooker, combine ribs, tomato, broth, wine, onion, horseradish, salt, pepper and ginger. Cover and cook on LOW 6 to 7 hours. Remove meat from cooker, cover, and keep warm. Turn control to HIGH. Dissolve cornstarch in water in a small bowl. Stir cornstarch mixture into cooker. Cover and cook on HIGH 15 to 20 minutes or until sauce is thickened. Spoon sauce over meat.

Beef Burgundy

Makes 6 servings

 A great classic made easy in your slow cooker.

3 bacon slices, chopped
2 lbs. beef sirloin tip or round steak, cut into 1-inch cubes
¼ cup all-purpose flour
½ teaspoon salt
½ teaspoon seasoned salt
½ teaspoon dried marjoram
½ teaspoon dried thyme
½ teaspoon pepper
2 cloves garlic, minced
1 beef bouillon cube, crushed
1 cup Burgundy wine
1 cup sliced fresh mushrooms
2 tablespoons cornstarch dissolved in 2 tablespoons water (optional)
Cooked wide noodles

In a large skillet, cook bacon several minutes. Remove bacon and set aside. Coat beef with flour and brown on all sides in bacon drippings. Combine beef, bacon drippings, cooked bacon, salt, seasoned salt, marjoram, thyme, pepper, garlic, bouillon and wine in a slow cooker. Cover and cook on LOW 6 to 8 hours or until beef is tender. Turn control to HIGH. Add mushrooms. Cover and cook on HIGH 15 minutes. To thicken sauce, if desired, add cornstarch mixture with mushrooms. Serve over noodles.

Teriyaki Steak
Makes 6 to 8 servings

 If fresh ginger is not available, use ¼ teaspoon ground ginger.

2 to 2½ lbs. boneless chuck steak
¼ cup soy sauce
1 (20-oz.) can unsweetened pineapple chunks, drained, and ¼ cup juice
    reserved
1 teaspoon finely grated gingerroot
1 tablespoon sugar
2 tablespoons vegetable oil
2 cloves garlic, crushed
3 tablespoons cornstarch
3 tablespoons water
Cooked rice

Cut meat into ⅛-inch slices and place in a slow cooker. In a small bowl, combine soy sauce, reserved pineapple juice, gingerroot, sugar, oil and garlic. Pour sauce mixture over meat. Cover and cook on LOW 6 to 7 hours. Turn control to HIGH. Stir in pineapple. Combine cornstarch and water in a small bowl; add to cooker. Cook, stirring, until slightly thickened. Serve over rice.

Chili con Carne

Makes 5 or 6 servings

Enjoy the flavors of a simple Mexican dish. Serve this colorful mixture of meat and vegetables with warm flour tortillas and salsa.

1½ lbs. beef stew meat
2 cloves garlic, crushed
½ teaspoon pepper
½ teaspoon salt
1 teaspoon chili powder
1 onion, chopped
1 teaspoon beef bouillon granules
1 (16-oz.) can sliced tomatoes with juice
1 (4-oz.) can green chiles, chopped
3 tablespoons chopped fresh cilantro
1 (16-oz.) can pinto beans, drained
Cooked rice

Sprinkle meat with garlic, pepper, salt and chili powder. Pat spices into meat. Cut meat into ½-inch cubes. Place meat in a slow cooker. Cover with onion, bouillon granules, tomatoes and chiles. Cover and cook on LOW 6 to 8 hours or until meat is tender. Turn control to HIGH. Add cilantro and beans. Cover and cook on HIGH 20 minutes. Serve on a bed of rice.

Farm-style Stew

Makes 5 or 6 servings

 Zucchini and corn give this basic stew a different look.

1½ lbs. beef stew meat, cut into 1-inch cubes
½ teaspoon pepper
1 teaspoon paprika
1 teaspoon seasoned salt
4 medium zucchini, cut crosswise into 1-inch-thick slices
1 cup hot water
2 tablespoons steak sauce
1 (17-oz.) can whole-kernel corn, drained
3 tablespoons cornstarch
3 tablespoons water

Sprinkle beef with pepper, paprika and seasoned salt. Place in a slow cooker with zucchini. Add hot water and steak sauce. Cover and cook on LOW 7 to 9 hours or until tender. Turn control to HIGH. Stir in corn. Dissolve cornstarch in water; add to meat mixture. Cover and cook on HIGH 15 to 20 minutes or until slightly thickened. Serve hot.

Hungarian Goulash

Makes 4 to 6 servings

Make this dish a day before you need it. The flavors improve and reheating does not adversely affect it.

1½ lbs. beef stew meat, cut into 1-inch cubes
1 large onion, chopped
2 cloves garlic, crushed
½ teaspoon salt
½ teaspoon pepper
½ cup water
2 tablespoons tomato paste
1 to 2 tablespoons sweet Hungarian paprika
¼ cup all-purpose flour
½ cup water
¼ cup sour cream or plain yogurt
Cooked noodles or rice
2 teaspoons dried dill weed or poppy seeds

Place meat in a slow cooker; cover with onion and garlic. In a small bowl, combine salt, pepper, water, tomato paste and paprika. Pour over meat mixture. Cover and cook on LOW 8 to 9 hours. Turn control to HIGH. In a small bowl, combine flour, water, and sour cream or yogurt. Stir into meat mixture. Cook uncovered on HIGH 10 to 15 minutes or until slightly thickened. Serve over cooked noodles or rice. Sprinkle with dill or poppy seeds.

Baja Beef 'n' Beans

Makes 5 or 6 servings

 The flavors of this dish are enhanced by salsa.

1½ lbs. boneless beef round steak
1 clove garlic, minced
¼ teaspoon pepper
¼ teaspoon salt
1 teaspoon chili powder
1 tablespoon prepared mustard
1 onion, chopped
1 teaspoon beef bouillon granules
1 cup fresh or bottled salsa
1 (16-oz.) can red or kidney beans, drained

Trim fat from meat. Combine garlic, pepper, salt, chili powder and mustard. Coat meat with mixture. Cut meat into ½-inch-wide strips. Place in a slow cooker. Stir in onion, bouillon granules and salsa. Cover and cook on LOW 7½ to 8 hours. Turn control to HIGH. Add beans. Cover and cook on HIGH 30 minutes.

Chinese Pepper Steak
Makes 4 to 6 servings

 Everyone clamors for this very colorful dish with its exotic flavors.

1 to 1½ lbs. boneless beef round steak
1 clove garlic, minced
½ teaspoon salt
¼ teaspoon pepper
¼ cup soy sauce
1 tablespoon hoisin sauce
1 teaspoon sugar
1 tomato, peeled, seeded and chopped
2 red or green bell peppers, cut into strips
3 tablespoons cornstarch
3 tablespoons water
1 cup fresh bean sprouts
4 green onions, finely chopped
Cooked rice

Trim fat from steak; slice into thin strips. Combine steak, garlic, salt, pepper, soy sauce, hoisin sauce and sugar in a slow cooker. Cover and cook on LOW about 4 hours. Turn control to HIGH. Add tomato and bell peppers. Dissolve cornstarch in water in a small bowl; stir into steak mixture. Cover and cook on HIGH 15 to 20 minutes or until thickened. Stir in bean sprouts. Sprinkle with onions. Serve with rice.

Swiss-style Beef Birds

Makes 5 or 6 servings

The combination of allspice, caraway seeds, and dill pickles creates a bold flavor. Carrot strips add a bright touch of color.

1½ lbs. beef round steak
1 teaspoon ground allspice
½ teaspoon caraway seeds
½ teaspoon salt
½ teaspoon pepper
2 medium carrots, peeled, halved and cut into strips
2 kosher dill pickles, cut into strips
¼ teaspoon garlic powder
1 (8-oz.) can tomato sauce
1 small onion, chopped
1 tablespoon all-purpose flour
3 tablespoons minced fresh parsley

With a mallet, pound beef to ¼-inch thickness. Sprinkle with allspice, caraway seeds, salt and pepper. Cut into 5 or 6 serving pieces. Place several carrot strips and 2 pickle strips on each piece of meat. Beginning at narrow end, roll up and secure with small skewers or wooden picks. Place meat in a slow cooker. In a small bowl, combine garlic powder, tomato sauce, onion and flour. Pour mixture over meat. Cover and cook on LOW 7 to 9 hours. Sprinkle with parsley before serving.

Creole-Asian Strips

Makes 5 or 6 servings

Two great cuisines are blended in one outstanding dish. Serve with rice or over noodles.

¼ teaspoon black pepper
¼ teaspoon red (cayenne) pepper
¼ teaspoon garlic powder
1 teaspoon dried tarragon leaves
½ teaspoon Chinese five spice powder
¼ teaspoon sugar
1½ lbs. beef flank steak, cut into ½-inch strips
½ green bell pepper, cut into strips
¾ cup chicken broth
2 bay leaves
3 tablespoons cornstarch
3 tablespoons water

In a small bowl, combine black pepper, cayenne pepper, garlic powder, tarragon, Chinese five spice powder and sugar. Sprinkle spice mixture over meat strips, patting and turning strips to coat both sides. Place meat in a slow cooker. Add bell pepper strips, chicken broth and bay leaves. Cover and cook on LOW 6 to 8 hours; remove bay leaves and discard. Dissolve cornstarch in water; stir into cooker. Turn control to HIGH. Cover and cook on HIGH 20 to 25 minutes or until thickened.

Flank Steak in Mushroom Wine Sauce

Makes 4 to 6 servings

A piquant wine sauce enhances the flavor of the steak; cut it into thin, diagonal strips before serving.

1 (1- to 1½-lb.) beef flank steak
¼ cup Sauterne wine
1 tablespoon soy sauce
1 clove garlic, minced
1 (10½-oz.) can condensed beef broth
1 tablespoon ketchup or tomato paste
1 tablespoon prepared mustard
1 small onion, finely chopped
3 tablespoons cornstarch
¼ cup water
¼ lb. fresh mushrooms, sliced

Place steak in a slow cooker. In a small bowl, combine wine, soy sauce, garlic, broth, ketchup or tomato paste, mustard and onion; pour mixture over steak. Cover and cook on LOW 6 to 7 hours. Turn control to HIGH. Dissolve cornstarch in water in a small bowl; stir into sauce in cooker. Add mushrooms. Cover and cook on HIGH 20 to 30 minutes or until mushrooms are tender. Slice meat in thin strips and serve with sauce.

Beef

Gingery Beef Strips
Makes 4 or 5 servings

 A pleasing one-dish meal with flavors from the Far East.

1 (1- to 1½-lb.) beef flank steak
1 (10½-oz.) can condensed beef broth
¼ cup soy sauce
1 teaspoon grated gingerroot
1 bunch green onions, sliced diagonally into 1-inch pieces
1 clove garlic, crushed
3 tablespoons cornstarch
2 tablespoons water
3 oz. Chinese pea pods
1½ cups fresh bean sprouts
Cooked rice

Thinly slice flank steak diagonally across the grain. In a slow cooker, combine steak, condensed broth, soy sauce, gingerroot, onions and garlic. Cover and cook on LOW 5 to 6 hours or until steak is tender. Turn control to HIGH. Dissolve cornstarch in water in a small bowl and stir into sauce in cooker. Cover and cook on HIGH 10 to 15 minutes or until thickened. During the last 5 minutes, drop in pea pods and bean sprouts. Serve over cooked rice.

Stuffed Flank Steak
with Currant Wine Sauce

Makes 4 or 5 servings

Flank steak becomes more flexible when it is scored, making it possible to roll up like a jellyroll.

1½ cups cubed bread stuffing
¾ cup sliced mushrooms (5 or 6 medium)
3 tablespoons water
2 tablespoons melted margarine or butter
2 tablespoons grated Parmesan cheese
1½ lbs. beef flank steak, scored on both sides
2 green onions, thinly sliced
¼ cup dry red wine
½ cup beef broth
2 tablespoons cornstarch dissolved in 2 tablespoons water
⅓ cup currant or grape jelly

In a medium bowl, combine stuffing, mushrooms, water, margarine or butter and cheese. Spread stuffing over steak; starting from a short end, roll up meat jellyroll style. Fasten with skewers or string. Place in a slow cooker. Top with green onions. Pour wine and beef broth over steak. Cover and cook on LOW about 7 hours or until meat is tender. Remove meat; turn control to HIGH. Stir cornstarch mixture into drippings in cooker. Cover and cook on HIGH 10 to 15 minutes or until thickened. Stir in currant or grape jelly. Cut meat into crosswise slices. Serve with sauce.

Old-Fashioned Beef Stew

Makes 6 to 8 servings

A long cooking time makes this a wonderful hot meal to come home to after a cold workday.

2 lbs. beef stew meat, cut into ½-inch cubes
1 bay leaf
1 tablespoon Worcestershire sauce
4 cups beef broth
¼ teaspoon pepper
½ teaspoon salt
1 teaspoon sugar
5 carrots, peeled and sliced or quartered
2 celery stalks, thinly sliced
4 potatoes, peeled and cut into eighths
15 to 20 white pearl onions, peeled
2 medium turnips, peeled and cut into eighths
¼ cup cornstarch
¼ cup water
1 (10-oz.) package frozen green peas, thawed

In a slow cooker, combine beef, bay leaf, Worcestershire sauce, 1 cup of the broth, pepper, salt, sugar, carrots, celery, potatoes, pearl onions and turnips. Pour remaining broth over beef and vegetables. Cover and cook on LOW 8 to 10 hours. Turn control to HIGH. Dissolve cornstarch in water; stir into beef mixture in cooker. Remove bay leaf. Add peas. Cover and cook on HIGH 10 to 15 minutes or until slightly thickened.

New England Chuck Roast

Makes 6 servings

A classic recipe with a savory sauce—just the thing for a large family or for company.

1 (3-lb.) beef chuck roast
1 teaspoon salt
¼ teaspoon pepper
1 onion, sliced
2 carrots, peeled and sliced
1 celery stalk, cut into 8 pieces
1 bay leaf
1 tablespoon vinegar
2 cups water
½ small cabbage, cut into wedges
3 tablespoons margarine or butter
1 tablespoon instant minced onion
2 tablespoons all-purpose flour
2 tablespoons prepared horseradish

Sprinkle meat with ½ teaspoon of the salt and the pepper. Place onion, carrots and celery in a slow cooker. Top with meat. Add bay leaf, vinegar and water. Cover and cook on LOW 5 to 7 hours or until meat is tender. Remove meat. Turn control to HIGH. Add cabbage wedges. Cover and cook on HIGH 15 to 20 minutes or until cabbage is done.

Meanwhile melt margarine or butter in a saucepan. Stir in instant onion and flour. Remove 1½ cups beef broth from slow cooker. Pour broth, horseradish and the remaining ½ teaspoon salt into saucepan. Cook over low heat, stirring constantly, until thickened and smooth. Serve roast and vegetables with the sauce.

Clockwise from top left: Padre Punch, page 17; Chicken & Leek Terrine, page 10; Cranberry Wine Punch, page 16; Mediterranean Caponata, page 9; and East Indian Snack, page 14

Clockwise from top left: Golden Squash Soup with Pesto Topping, page 36; Tortilla Soup, page 43; and Fennel-Bean Soup, page 27

Clockwise from top: Homestead Ham Loaf, page 96; Spicy Brisket over Noodles, page 66; and Swedish Cabbage Rolls, page 73

Clockwise from top: Red & Gold Sweet-Sour Chicken, page 139; Southeast Asian–style Meatballs, page 150; and Chinese Pepper Steak, page 83

Beef Stroganoff

Makes 6 or 7 servings

The taste of this homemade dish beats packaged mixes any day. You can leave it cooking while you are at work, and it takes just minutes to complete once you get home.

1½ to 2 lbs. round steak
½ teaspoon salt
⅛ teaspoon pepper
1 onion, sliced
¼ teaspoon garlic salt
1 tablespoon Worcestershire sauce
½ teaspoon paprika
1 (10½-oz.) can condensed beef broth
1 tablespoon ketchup
2 tablespoons dry red wine
¼ lb. fresh mushrooms, sliced
3 tablespoons cornstarch
¼ cup water
1 cup sour cream
Cooked rice or noodles

Cut steak into ¼-inch strips. Season with salt and pepper. Place steak and onion in a slow cooker. Mix garlic salt, Worcestershire sauce, paprika, broth and ketchup in a bowl. Pour mixture over steak. Cover and cook on LOW 6 to 7 hours or until steak is tender. Turn control to HIGH. Add wine and mushrooms. Dissolve cornstarch in water in a small bowl. Add to meat mixture, stirring until blended. Cover and cook on HIGH 15 minutes or until slightly thickened. Stir in sour cream; turn off heat. Serve with rice or noodles.

Pork & Lamb

New recipes like Hawaiian Pork Chops, Indonesian Pork, and Fruited Lamb Roll take advantage of the increasing popularity of pork and lamb. When it comes to a choice of meats for your slow cooker, the sky is the limit. Or, use your slow cooker for variations of old favorites. This way you can add new variety to your menus with less effort.

Spareribs cook especially well in the slow cooker. They come out oh so tender. Some tempting sparerib recipes you'll love include Barbecued Spareribs, Chinese-style Country Ribs and Buck County's Spareribs.

Be sure to check the meat at the minimum suggested cooking time. Let it cook longer if necessary to suit your own taste buds. With a little experience you will develop a "feel" for the time needed for the exact degree of doneness you like.

Meat recipes combined with vegetables will keep your meat-hungry family happy while allowing you to stay out of the kitchen until the last few minutes before dinner.

Some larger roasts will only fit into 4- or 5-quart and larger cookers.

You may want to use a meat thermometer with these just as you would when cooking in the oven. If yours is a 3½-quart or smaller cooker, use a small-size roast and/or have the butcher remove any bones and tie the meat to make it more compact. Remember: Smaller roasts take slightly less cooking time.

You will have more meat juices when you finish than you would with other cooking methods. Make the most of the wonderful flavor these juices contain by spooning them over slices of the meat, or by thickening them with flour or cornstarch dissolved in a little water. Pass the gravy to serve over pasta, rice or potatoes.

Pork—"To brown or not to brown"?—that is the question. It's a good idea to brown spareribs before cooking them in a slow cooker. Choose meaty ribs, lightly brown them in the oven or broiler and drain the excess fat before adding sauce and vegetables. If pork steaks and chops are fairly lean, either brown them or just trim the excess fat off the edges.

The same principle applies to lamb. If there is fat, trim off the excess or brown the meat and drain off the fat before placing it in your slow cooker. You may want to pour off or skim off the fat at least once during the cooking process.

Indonesian Pork

Makes 5 to 6 servings

A tangy sauce that's slightly sweet and spicy is sparked with a little heat from dried red pepper flakes.

1 (4- to 5-lb.) pork roast
Salt and pepper to taste
¼ cup honey
¼ cup soy sauce
½ teaspoon dried red pepper flakes
¼ cup fresh lemon juice
1 tablespoon chopped crystallized ginger
¾ cup crunchy peanut butter

Place a metal rack or trivet in the bottom of a slow cooker. Place meat on rack. Sprinkle with salt and pepper. In a small bowl, combine honey, soy sauce, pepper flakes and lemon juice. Pour mixture over meat. Sprinkle ginger over meat. Cover and cook on LOW 9 to 10 hours. Remove meat and keep warm. Skim off excess fat from juices. Turn control to HIGH. Stir in peanut butter and cook about 5 minutes. Slice meat and serve with sauce.

Homestead Ham Loaf

Makes 6 to 8 servings

 A loaf that slices beautifully and makes a wonderful sandwich filling.

3 cups ground cooked ham
8 oz. bulk pork sausage
3 green onions, chopped
1 cup rolled oats
1 celery stalk, chopped
¼ cup chopped fresh parsley
1 egg, slightly beaten
½ cup milk
2 tablespoons Dijon mustard
1 teaspoon prepared horseradish

In a large bowl, combine ham, sausage, green onions, oats, celery, parsley, egg and milk. Form into a 6-inch round loaf or a 9 × 5-inch oval. Place in a slow cooker. Cover and cook on LOW 6 to 7 hours. Combine mustard and horseradish and spread over ham loaf. Slice loaf and serve.

NOTE: Ham can be cut into chunks and ground in a food processor or meat grinder.

Chinese-style Country Ribs
Makes 4 to 6 servings

Soy sauce and orange marmalade are combined to give these ribs a different flavor.

¼ cup soy sauce
¼ cup orange marmalade
2 tablespoons ketchup
1 clove garlic, crushed

3 to 4 lbs. country-style or regular pork spareribs, cut into 2-rib pieces

In a small bowl, combine soy sauce, marmalade, ketchup and garlic. Brush both sides of ribs with mixture. Place in a slow cooker. Pour remaining sauce over ribs. Cover and cook on LOW 8 to 10 hours or until ribs are tender. Serve hot.

Buck County's Spareribs
Makes 4 to 5 servings

Brown spareribs in the oven; then discard drippings before combining with other ingredients in slow cooker.

2½ to 3 lbs. spareribs
1 teaspoon salt
¼ teaspoon pepper

1 (1-lb.) can sauerkraut, drained
1 apple, cored and diced
1 tablespoon sugar

Preheat oven to 400F (205C). Cut spareribs into serving-size pieces. Sprinkle with salt and pepper. Place on a rack in a baking pan. Brown in oven 15 minutes; turn and brown other side about 10 to 15 minutes. Pour off fat. Spoon sauerkraut into bottom of a slow cooker. Top with apple; sprinkle sugar over apple. Place ribs on top. Cover and cook on LOW 5½ to 6 hours or until ribs are tender. Serve hot.

Soy-Glazed Spareribs

Makes 5 to 6 servings

Honey, soy sauce and pineapple juice are blended into a delightful glaze. Finger licking is permitted when eating these morsels.

4 to 5 lbs. spareribs, cut into 2-rib pieces
Salt and pepper to taste
½ cup pineapple juice
2 tablespoons garlic-flavored wine vinegar
¼ cup dry white wine
2 tablespoons soy sauce
2 tablespoons honey
½ cup chicken broth
2 tablespoons cornstarch
3 tablespoons water

Preheat oven to 400F (205C). Place spareribs on a rack in a shallow baking pan. Brown in oven 15 minutes; turn and brown on other side 10 to 15 minutes. Drain fat. Sprinkle ribs with salt and pepper. Place ribs in a slow cooker. In a small bowl, combine pineapple juice, vinegar, wine, soy sauce, honey and broth; pour mixture over ribs. Cover and cook on LOW 7 to 9 hours. Turn control to HIGH. In a small bowl, dissolve cornstarch in water; stir into rib mixture. Cover and cook on HIGH 10 to 15 minutes or until slightly thickened. Serve hot.

Barbecued Spareribs

Makes 5 to 7 servings

 This is a very popular barbecue sauce for traditional spareribs.

4 to 5 lbs. spareribs, cut into 2-rib pieces
1 cup ketchup
2 to 3 drops hot pepper sauce
¼ cup vinegar
¼ cup packed brown sugar
½ teaspoon salt
1 teaspoon celery seeds
1 small onion, finely chopped

Preheat oven to 400F (205C). Place spareribs on a rack in a shallow baking pan. Brown in oven 15 minutes; turn and brown on other side 10 to 15 minutes. Drain fat. Place ribs in a slow cooker. In a small bowl, combine ketchup, pepper sauce, vinegar, brown sugar, salt, celery seeds, and onion. Pour mixture over ribs; turn ribs until evenly coated. Cover and cook on LOW about 6 hours or until ribs are tender. Serve hot.

Rio Grande Country Ribs
Makes 5 to 6 servings

 Warm flour tortillas make a perfect accompaniment to this hearty dish.

2½ to 3 lbs. country-style pork ribs
1 onion, thinly sliced
1 (7-oz.) can green chile salsa
¼ cup dry white wine
3 tablespoons brown sugar
1 tablespoon Worcestershire sauce
1 teaspoon prepared mustard
½ teaspoon chili powder
2 tablespoons cornstarch
3 tablespoons water
⅓ cup sour cream
1 tablespoon chopped fresh cilantro

Combine ribs and onion in a slow cooker. In a medium bowl, combine salsa, wine, brown sugar, Worcestershire sauce, mustard and chili powder. Pour mixture over meat. Cover and cook on LOW 6 to 7 hours or until ribs are tender. Remove ribs from cooker and keep warm. Turn control to HIGH. In a small bowl, dissolve cornstarch in water; stir into drippings in cooker. Cover and cook on HIGH 15 to 20 minutes or until slightly thickened. Spoon sauce over ribs. Top each serving with a dollop of sour cream and sprinkle with cilantro.

Rathskeller Pork

Makes 5 servings

Inspired by an old German family recipe, this is an autumn favorite at our house. Remove cooked pork and cabbage with a slotted spoon, leaving liquid in the cooker.

5 pork steaks or chops, about ¾ inch thick
2 cups shredded red cabbage
2 green onions, chopped
2 apples, peeled, cored and sliced
3 tablespoons apple jelly
2 tablespoons white wine vinegar
1 teaspoon seasoned salt
¼ teaspoon seasoned pepper
½ teaspoon caraway seeds

Trim all visible fat from pork. In a large bowl, combine cabbage, onions, apples, apple jelly, vinegar, seasoned salt, seasoned pepper and caraway seeds. Place cabbage mixture in a slow cooker; top with pork. Cover and cook on LOW 4½ to 5 hours or until pork is tender.

Autumn Pork Chops

Makes 6 servings

 The sauce adds an appetizing golden-brown look to the chops and squash.

6 pork chops, about ½ inch thick
1 medium acorn squash, unpeeled
½ teaspoon salt
2 tablespoons margarine or butter, melted
¾ cup packed brown sugar
¾ teaspoon Kitchen Bouquet browning and seasoning sauce
⅛ teaspoon freshly grated nutmeg
2 tablespoons orange juice
1 teaspoon grated orange peel

Trim fat from edges of chops. Cut squash into 6 crosswise slices. Arrange 3 chops on bottom of a slow cooker. Top with the squash slices; add remaining 3 chops. In a small bowl, combine salt, margarine or butter, brown sugar, browning sauce, nutmeg, orange juice and orange peel. Spoon mixture over chops. Cover and cook on LOW 5 to 5½ hours or until pork chops are tender. Serve a slice of squash along with each pork chop.

Corn-Stuffed Pork Chops
Makes 5 to 6 servings

Green peppers and sun-dried tomatoes make a colorful stuffing for these pork chops, which are especially good with fruit salad and lemon-buttered broccoli.

5 or 6 pork chops, 1½ to 2 inches thick
1 (8-oz.) can whole-kernel corn, drained, liquid reserved
1 cup seasoned bread stuffing mix
2 tablespoons finely chopped onion
2 tablespoons minced green bell pepper
½ teaspoon salt
¼ cup chopped sun-dried tomatoes in oil, drained
2 tablespoons chopped fresh basil
4 teaspoons cornstarch
1 tablespoon water

Have the butcher cut a pocket in each pork chop, or use a sharp knife to cut a horizontal slit in the side of each chop, forming a pocket for stuffing. In a medium bowl, mix corn, 3 tablespoons reserved liquid from corn, stuffing mix, onion, bell pepper, salt, sun-dried tomatoes and basil. Stir until liquid is absorbed. Spoon corn mixture into pockets in chops. Close with wooden picks or small skewers. Place a metal rack or trivet in a slow cooker. Place chops on rack. Cover and cook on LOW 6 to 7 hours or until pork chops are tender. Turn slow cooker to HIGH. Remove chops and rack. Dissolve cornstarch in water. Stir into cooking juices. Cover and cook about 15 minutes, stirring at least once. Spoon sauce over chops.

Hawaiian Pork Chops

Makes 6 servings

You will think you are in the South Seas when you taste this tropical combination of fruit and nuts.

6 lean boneless pork chops or cutlets
1 tablespoon prepared mustard
2 tablespoons white wine vinegar
1 tablespoon hoisin sauce
½ teaspoon salt
⅛ teaspoon pepper
1 (8-oz.) can pineapple chunks in juice
2 tablespoons cornstarch
2 tablespoons water
1 papaya, peeled, seeded and sliced
Toasted coconut and/or chopped macadamia nuts

Place chops in a slow cooker. In a small bowl, combine mustard, vinegar, hoisin sauce, salt and pepper. Drain juice from pineapple and add juice to mustard mixture; reserve pineapple chunks. Pour sauce over chops in cooker. Cover and cook on LOW 5 to 6 hours or until meat is tender. Remove chops and keep warm. Turn control to HIGH. Dissolve cornstarch in water in a small bowl; stir cornstarch mixture into juices in cooker. Cover and cook on HIGH 10 to 15 minutes. Stir in pineapple chunks and papaya. Serve chops accompanied by sauce and let each diner add coconut or macadamias as desired.

Plantation Pork Chops

Makes 4 servings

It is important to purchase extra-thick pork chops so you have an adequate pocket for stuffing.

4 loin pork chops, about 1½ inches thick
1½ cups dry cornbread stuffing
2 tablespoons margarine or butter, melted
⅓ cup orange juice
1 tablespoon finely chopped pecans
¼ cup light corn syrup
½ teaspoon freshly grated orange peel
¼ teaspoon salt
⅛ teaspoon pepper
1 tablespoon cornstarch
1 tablespoon water

Have the butcher cut a pocket in each pork chop, or use a sharp knife to cut a horizontal slit in the side of each chop, forming a pocket for stuffing. Combine stuffing, margarine or butter, orange juice and pecans. Fill pockets with stuffing. Place a metal rack in a slow cooker. Place chops on rack. In a small bowl, combine corn syrup, orange peel, salt and pepper. Brush mixture over pork chops. Cover and cook on LOW about 6 hours.

Turn control to HIGH. Remove chops and rack from cooker and keep chops warm. Dissolve cornstarch in water in a small bowl; stir into liquid in cooker. Cover and cook on HIGH 15 to 20 minutes. Spoon sauce over cooked chops.

Cranberry Pork Roast

Makes 6 to 8 servings

 Tart cranberries and honey accent the delicate flavor of pork roast.

1 (3- to 4-lb.) boneless or loin pork roast
Salt and pepper to taste
1 cup ground or finely chopped cranberries
¼ cup honey
1 teaspoon freshly grated orange peel
⅛ teaspoon ground cloves
⅛ teaspoon freshly grated nutmeg

Sprinkle roast with salt and pepper. Place in a slow cooker. In a small bowl, combine remaining ingredients; pour over roast. Cover and cook on LOW 8 to 10 hours or until roast is tender. Slice and serve hot.

Black Bean Chili with Pork

Makes 6 to 8 servings

 This colorful, hearty main dish offers a cool contrast with its yogurt topping.

1 lb. boneless pork, cut into ½-inch cubes
2 (16-oz.) cans black beans, drained
1 red or yellow bell pepper, chopped
1 medium tomato, peeled, seeded and chopped
1 small red onion, thinly sliced
1 clove garlic, crushed
½ teaspoon ground cumin
2 teaspoons chili powder
½ teaspoon salt
1 (8-oz.) can tomato sauce
½ cup plain low-fat yogurt or sour cream
2 tablespoons chopped cilantro leaves

In a slow cooker, stir together pork, beans, bell pepper, tomato, onion, garlic, cumin, chili powder, salt and tomato sauce. Cover and cook on LOW 8 to 9 hours. Spoon into individual bowls; top with yogurt and cilantro.

Crockery Ham

Makes 8 to 10 servings

 Add a festive touch to ham with this spicy currant sauce.

1 (5- to 7-lb.) cooked ham (with or without bone, butt or shank half)
Whole cloves
½ cup currant jelly
1 tablespoon vinegar
½ teaspoon dry mustard
¼ teaspoon ground cinnamon

Place a metal rack or trivet in a 4-quart or larger slow cooker. Place ham on rack. Cover and cook on LOW 5 to 6 hours. Remove ham. Pour off juices; remove skin and fat. Score ham; stud with whole cloves. In a small saucepan, melt jelly with vinegar, mustard and cinnamon. Remove metal rack or trivet. Return ham to slow cooker. Spoon sauce over ham. Cover and cook on HIGH 20 to 30 minutes, brushing with sauce at least once (several times if possible). Slice and serve hot or cold.

Knockwurst with Hot German Potato Salad

Makes 4 servings

 Potatoes are paired with bacon and sausage and topped with a pleasing sauce.

4 large potatoes
1 onion, sliced
Water
4 bacon slices, diced
2 tablespoons all-purpose flour
2 tablespoons sugar
1 teaspoon dry mustard
½ teaspoon salt
¼ teaspoon pepper
⅓ cup vinegar
⅔ cup water
½ teaspoon celery seeds
4 knockwurst links
1 tablespoon finely chopped fresh parsley

Peel and slice potatoes. Combine potatoes with onion in a slow cooker. Cover with water. Cover and cook on LOW 5 to 6 hours or on HIGH 2 to 3 hours. Remove from cooker; drain thoroughly and return to cooker. Meanwhile, cook bacon in a skillet over medium heat. Stir in flour, sugar, mustard, salt and pepper; mix well. Add vinegar, ⅔ cup water and celery seeds. Cook several minutes or until thickened. Pour over drained potatoes in slow cooker. Top with knockwurst. Turn control to HIGH. Cover and cook on HIGH 30 to 40 minutes or until mixture is hot. Sprinkle with parsley.

Kielbasa & Napa Cabbage

Makes 6 servings

The shape of Napa or Chinese cabbage is similar to that of romaine lettuce, but it is off-white or a very pale green color. If not available, use regular cabbage.

1 lb. kielbasa (Polish sausage)
1 onion, thinly sliced
1 small head Napa cabbage, coarsely shredded
2 apples, peeled, cored and sliced
½ teaspoon salt
1 teaspoon caraway seeds
2 cups chicken broth

Cut kielbasa into 2-inch chunks. In a slow cooker, arrange alternate layers of sausage with onion, cabbage and apples. Sprinkle with salt and caraway seeds. Add broth. Cover and cook on LOW 5 to 6 hours or until cabbage is tender. Serve with a slotted spoon to drain off liquid.

Fruited Lamb Roll

Makes 6 to 8 servings

Apricots and cranberries plump up in this moist, flavorful roast. Let the meat rest, covered, 10 to 15 minutes before serving.

1 (3- to 4-lb.) rolled boneless lamb roast
3 cloves garlic, crushed
¼ cup minced gingerroot
½ cup dried cranberries
6 oz. dried apricots
2 tablespoons chopped fresh mint leaves

Open rolled roast. Sprinkle with garlic, gingerroot and cranberries. Arrange apricots in a single layer over roast. Sprinkle mint over apricots. Roll roast tightly and secure with string or skewers. Place roast on a rack in a slow cooker. Cover and cook on LOW 8 to 10 hours or until lamb is tender. Slice and serve hot.

Marinated Leg of Lamb

Makes 8 to 10 servings

This size roast will not fit into a small slow cooker; it must be boned or cooked in a 5-quart cooker.

1 (5- to 6-lb.) leg of lamb
2 cloves garlic
¼ cup kosher or coarse salt
2 tablespoons peppercorns, cracked
¼ cup cognac or brandy
2 cups dry red wine

Trim excess fat from lamb. Cut each garlic clove into 4 to 6 slices. Using a paring knife, make small slits in various places in the meat and insert the garlic slivers. Sprinkle salt and pepper over all sides of the lamb. Place meat in a large bowl; pour cognac or brandy over it. Refrigerate several hours or overnight, brushing with cognac or brandy and turning several times.

Drain meat; place in a slow cooker with wine. Cover and cook on LOW 9 to 10 hours or until meat is done. If possible turn roast once during cooking. Cut into thin slices.

Algerian Lamb Shanks
Makes 5 to 6 servings

Fruits and meat are often combined in North African dishes. Serve this lamb mixture over couscous.

4 lamb shanks
1 teaspoon salt
¼ teaspoon pepper
1 cup dried apricots
½ cup pitted prunes
½ cup slivered almonds
½ cup water
½ cup orange juice
2 tablespoons vinegar
1 teaspoon ground allspice
1 teaspoon ground cinnamon
½ teaspoon ground cloves
Cooked couscous or rice

Coat lamb shanks with salt and pepper. Place in a slow cooker with meaty ends down. Add apricots, prunes and almonds. In a small bowl, combine water, orange juice, vinegar, allspice, cinnamon and cloves. Pour over meat and fruits. Cover and cook on LOW 7 to 9 hours or until meat is very tender. Remove meat from bones and return meat to cooker to reheat. Serve meat on a bed of couscous or rice.

Greek Herbed Lamb with Rice

Makes 4 to 6 servings

Traditional Greek flavors, including mint, oregano, and garlic, highlight this ethnic treat.

4 lamb shanks
1 cup white wine
1 tablespoon dried oregano, crushed
1 tablespoon dried mint, crushed
1 teaspoon green peppercorns, crushed
¼ teaspoon salt
2 cloves garlic, minced
1 cup uncooked rice

Place lamb shanks in a slow cooker with meaty ends down. In a small bowl, combine wine, oregano, mint, peppercorns, salt and garlic. Pour mixture over lamb. Cover and cook on LOW 7 to 9 hours or until meat is tender. Remove meat from bones; discard bones. Return meat to cooker. Turn control to HIGH. Add rice; cover and cook 1 hour.

Mexican Lamb with Red Wine
Makes 6 servings

Authentic Mexican flavor is easy with readily available chili powder and a few herbs.

4 lamb shanks
1 cup red wine
¼ cup chili powder
½ teaspoon ground ginger
1 teaspoon ground cumin
1 teaspoon dried oregano
2 cloves garlic, minced
¼ teaspoon salt
Rice or tortillas
Salsa

Place lamb in a slow cooker with meaty ends down. In a small bowl, combine wine, chili powder, ginger, cumin, oregano, garlic and salt. Pour mixture over lamb shanks. Cover and cook on LOW 7 to 9 hours or until meat is very tender. Remove meat from bones; discard bones. Return meat to liquid. Serve over rice or wrap in warm tortillas with salsa.

Irish Lamb Stew

Makes 5 to 6 servings

 The rich flavor of lamb is enhanced with herbs and vegetables.

1½ lbs. lamb stew meat, cut into 1-inch cubes
1 onion, chopped
1 cup beef broth
3 medium potatoes, peeled and chopped
1 celery stalk, chopped
½ teaspoon salt
¼ teaspoon pepper
½ teaspoon dried marjoram
¼ teaspoon dried thyme leaves
1 (10-oz.) package frozen green peas, thawed
3 tablespoons cornstarch
¼ cup water
2 tablespoons chopped fresh parsley

Combine meat, onion, beef broth, potatoes, celery, salt, pepper, marjoram and thyme in a slow cooker. Cover and cook on LOW 8 to 10 hours or until meat and potatoes are tender. Turn control to HIGH. Add peas. In a small bowl, dissolve cornstarch in water; stir into stew. Cover and cook 15 to 20 minutes or until slightly thickened. Stir in parsley.

Poultry

New recipes featuring some of the latest flavor combinations are included in the poultry section. For a California taste try Mission Chicken with grapes, orange juice, cinnamon, cloves and lemon pepper. Or, how about Curried Island Chicken, Thai Chicken, Arroz con Pollo or Southeast Asian–style Meatballs. If you like your food very spicy, there's the popular Caribbean "Jerked" Chicken. Many of the recipes take advantage of chicken's mild flavor, adding sun-dried tomatoes, mushrooms, more spices and herbs, even wine.

Poultry is today's most popular meat. In the slow cooker chicken generally takes less time to cook than other meats and comes out tender and moist.

You will find many variations of family favorites using whole chickens. Other recipes, such as Cashew Chicken and Tarragon Chicken Thighs, use broiler halves or quarters, cut-up chicken parts or cooked chunks of chicken and are equally delicious in your slow cooker. Naturally, the larger whole birds require longer cooking times than the bite-size pieces.

Carrots, eggplant, celery and potatoes can take longer to cook than chicken. Be sure the vegetables are covered with liquid such as water, bouillon or tomato sauce. Also, you may want to place the vegetables on the bottom of the pot with the chicken on top. This way, the vegetables cook more evenly and should be done about the same time as the chicken.

For a change of pace, you'll like the way turkey parts taste when slow cooked. Turkey legs, thighs and wings lend themselves especially well to this cooking method. They are tender, juicy and very flavorful. Larger turkey parts fit into 4-quart or larger pots. If you have a 3½-quart pot, buy the smaller parts or remove the bones so the turkey will fit. Turkey Lasagna and Short-Cut Turkey Chili are just two of the many dishes for ground turkey.

Rounding out the poultry section are recipes for Cornish Hens with Cherry Sauce, Cornish Hens with Lime Glaze, and two delicious ways to prepare duckling.

Cashew Chicken
Makes 5 or 6 servings

For an appetizing and colorful addition to this recipe, garnish each serving with thin slices of mango.

6 boneless skinless chicken breast halves, cut into 1-inch strips (optional)
4 to 5 mushrooms, sliced
3 green onions, sliced into ½-inch pieces
¼ cup soy sauce
2 teaspoons grated gingerroot
½ cup chicken broth
¼ teaspoon salt
⅛ teaspoon pepper
1 (8-oz.) can sliced bamboo shoots, drained
½ cup cashews, toasted (see Note, page 9)
½ cup Chinese pea pods
2 tablespoons cornstarch
3 tablespoons water
Cooked rice

Place chicken and mushrooms in a slow cooker. Add green onions, soy sauce, gingerroot, broth, salt and pepper. Cover and cook on LOW about 4 hours. Add bamboo shoots, cashews and pea pods; turn control to HIGH. In a small bowl, dissolve cornstarch in water. Stir into chicken mixture in cooker. Cover and cook on HIGH 20 to 30 minutes or until thickened, stirring at least once. Serve over cooked rice.

Caribbean "Jerked" Chicken

Makes 5 servings

To crisp the "jerked" coating on the cooked chicken, broil or grill for several minutes or until bubbly.

½ cup sliced green onions
2 tablespoons grated gingerroot
1 teaspoon ground allspice
3 fresh jalapeño chiles, seeded and coarsely chopped
1 teaspoon vegetable oil
2 teaspoons seasoned pepper
½ teaspoon salt
1 clove garlic
1 tablespoon honey
5 chicken thighs and drumsticks (joined together)
Cooked rice
Papaya (optional), peeled and sliced

In a blender or food processor, combine onions, gingerroot, allspice, jalapeño chiles, oil, seasoned pepper, salt and garlic. Process until finely chopped. Stir in honey to form a paste. Brush on all sides of chicken. Place a rack in a slow cooker. Place chicken on rack. Cover and cook on LOW 4 to 4½ hours or until chicken is tender. Serve with rice. Garnish with papaya.

Kowloon Chicken

Makes 5 or 6 servings

The success of this popular dish depends on the contrast of the ginger and soy with the sweet mango flavor.

3 to 3½ lbs. chicken parts
1 teaspoon grated gingerroot
1 clove garlic, minced
1 cup chicken broth
¼ teaspoon salt
⅛ teaspoon pepper
1 mango, peeled and diced
1 (4-oz.) can sliced water chestnuts, drained
4 green onions, diagonally sliced
¼ cup cornstarch
¼ cup soy sauce
Cooked rice or noodles

Place chicken in a slow cooker. In a small bowl, combine gingerroot, garlic, broth, salt and pepper. Pour mixture over chicken. Cover and cook on LOW 4½ to 5 hours or until chicken is tender. Turn control to HIGH. Add mango, water chestnuts, and green onions. In a small bowl, dissolve cornstarch in soy sauce; stir into cooking juices in cooker. Cover and cook on HIGH 15 to 20 minutes or until slightly thickened. Serve with cooked rice or noodles.

Chicken Cacciatore

Makes 5 or 6 servings

For a change serve this dish over strands of steamed spaghetti squash. The texture and colors are great together.

1 (2½- to 3½-lb.) broiler-fryer chicken, cut up
1 onion, chopped
1 teaspoon dried basil or oregano
½ teaspoon lemon pepper
¼ teaspoon salt
2 garlic cloves, minced
¼ cup rosé wine
1 tablespoon sugar
½ green bell pepper, sliced
1 (8-oz.) can tomato sauce
1 cup sliced fresh mushrooms
Cooked pasta

Combine all ingredients except mushrooms and pasta in a slow cooker. Cover and cook on LOW 5 to 6 hours. Turn control to HIGH and add mushrooms. Cover and cook about 10 minutes. Serve over pasta.

Venetian Chicken

Makes 5 or 6 servings

 Robust flavors of sun-dried tomatoes and mushrooms complement chicken.

1 teaspoon sweet paprika
¼ cup all-purpose flour
1 teaspoon dried basil
¼ teaspoon salt
¼ teaspoon pepper
1 (2½- to 3½-lb.) broiler-fryer chicken, cut up
3 to 4 dried mushrooms
¼ cup chopped sun-dried tomatoes
1 small onion, chopped
2 tablespoons red wine (optional)
1 (8-oz.) can tomato sauce
1 tablespoon freshly grated lemon peel
Cooked pasta
Grated Parmesan cheese
Chopped fresh parsley

In a large bowl, combine paprika, flour, basil, salt and pepper. Coat chicken pieces with mixture; set aside. Rinse mushrooms and break into small pieces; remove and discard thick stems. Place mushrooms, sun-dried tomatoes and onion in a slow cooker. Place chicken pieces on top. In a bowl, combine wine, if using, tomato sauce and lemon peel; pour over chicken. Cover and cook on LOW 5 to 6 hours or until chicken is tender. Serve over pasta; top with Parmesan cheese and parsley.

Chicken Breasts, Saltimbocca Style
Makes 6 chicken rolls

 My version of a famous Italian dish.

6 boneless skinless chicken breast halves
6 small slices ham
6 small slices Swiss cheese
¼ cup all-purpose flour
¼ cup grated Parmesan cheese
1 teaspoon salt
½ teaspoon ground dried sage
¼ teaspoon pepper
⅓ cup vegetable oil
1 (10½-oz.) can condensed cream of chicken soup
½ cup dry white wine
¼ cup cornstarch
¼ cup water
Cooked rice

Pound chicken breast halves until thin between two sheets of waxed paper or foil. Place a slice of ham and cheese on each chicken piece. Roll up and tuck ends in; secure with small skewers or wooden picks. Combine flour, Parmesan cheese, salt, sage and pepper in a shallow bowl. Coat chicken rolls in flour mixture. Refrigerate chicken at least 1 hour.

In a large skillet, heat oil over medium heat. Add chicken rolls and cook, turning, until browned on all sides. Place browned chicken in a slow cooker. Combine soup and wine and pour over chicken rolls. Cover and cook on LOW 4 to 5 hours or until chicken is tender. Turn control to HIGH. In a small bowl, dissolve cornstarch in water; stir into cooking juices in cooker. Cover and cook on HIGH 10 minutes. Serve with hot rice.

Sorrento Chicken Roll-ups

Makes 6 servings

Entertaining is a breeze when you prepare these roll-ups ahead of time; let them cook while you are busy with other chores.

6 boneless skinless chicken breast halves
6 slices prosciutto
2 tablespoons Dijon mustard
½ teaspoon ground dried sage
½ teaspoon salt
⅛ teaspoon pepper
¼ cup dry white wine
½ cup chicken broth
¾ cup chopped mushrooms
3 tablespoons cornstarch
½ cup milk or half-and-half
Cooked pasta or rice

Place chicken between 2 sheets of waxed paper or foil. Pound with a meat mallet until about ½ inch thick. Place each chicken piece on a prosciutto slice. Spread top of each chicken piece with mustard and sprinkle with sage. Starting at short end, roll up each "sandwich" jellyroll style. Place in a slow cooker. Sprinkle with salt and pepper. Add wine and broth. Cover and cook on LOW 5 to 6 hours. Remove chicken rolls and keep warm. Add mushrooms to cooking juices in cooker. Turn control to HIGH. In a small bowl, dissolve cornstarch in milk or half-and-half; stir into mushroom mixture in cooker. Cover and cook on HIGH 20 to 30 minutes or until thickened, stirring once. Serve chicken rolls over pasta or rice. Top each serving with sauce.

Chicken Tetrazzini

Makes 5 or 6 servings

The chicken absorbs interesting flavors from other ingredients in the slow cooker. Add finishing touches at the last minute.

4 boneless skinless chicken breast halves, cut into 2 × ½-inch strips
1 cup chicken broth
½ cup dry white wine
1 onion, finely chopped
½ teaspoon salt
¼ teaspoon dried thyme
¼ teaspoon pepper
2 tablespoons minced fresh parsley
6 to 8 mushrooms, sliced
3 tablespoons cornstarch
¼ cup water
½ cup half-and-half
8 oz. spaghetti, broken into 2-inch pieces, cooked and drained
½ cup grated Parmesan cheese

In a slow cooker, combine chicken, broth, wine, onion, salt, thyme, pepper and parsley. Cover and cook on LOW 4 to 5 hours. Turn control to HIGH. Add mushrooms. In a small bowl, dissolve cornstarch in water; stir into slow cooker. Cover and cook on HIGH 20 minutes. Stir in half-and-half, cooked spaghetti, and half the cheese. Cover and heat on HIGH 5 to 10 minutes. Spoon into serving dish; sprinkle with remaining cheese.

Arroz con Pollo

Makes 4 to 5 servings

 A delightful chicken and rice dish from Spain and Mexico is very popular here.

½ teaspoon salt
¼ teaspoon pepper
1 clove garlic, crushed
1 teaspoon dried oregano
2 teaspoons chili powder
1 (2½- to 3½-lb.) broiler-fryer chicken, cut up
½ cup chicken broth
2 tablespoons red wine
1 (10-oz.) package frozen green peas, thawed
½ cup pimiento-stuffed olives
2 cups cooked rice
2 tablespoons chopped fresh cilantro

In a small bowl, combine salt, pepper, garlic, oregano and chili powder. Sprinkle spice mixture over both sides of chicken pieces. Place chicken in a slow cooker. Pour broth and wine over chicken. Cover and cook on LOW 5 to 6 hours. Remove chicken and cover to keep warm. Turn control to HIGH. Add peas and olives. Cover and cook on HIGH 7 to 10 minutes. Stir in cooked rice and chicken until combined. Sprinkle with cilantro and serve.

Chicken Olé

Makes 8 servings

Try this creamy casserole that's highlighted with fresh orange and avocado slices.

1 (10¾-oz.) can condensed cream of chicken soup
1 (10¾-oz.) can condensed cream of mushroom soup
1 (7-oz.) can green chile salsa
1 cup sour cream
1 tablespoon grated onion
12 corn tortillas, cut into 6 or 8 pieces each
4 cups coarsely chopped cooked chicken or turkey
¾ cup (3 oz.) shredded Cheddar cheese
Orange slices
Avocado slices

Lightly grease sides and bottom of a slow cooker. Combine soups, salsa, sour cream and onion in a bowl. In the slow cooker, arrange alternating layers of tortillas with chicken and soup mixture. Cover and cook on LOW 4 to 5 hours. Sprinkle with cheese. Cover and cook on LOW another 5 or 10 minutes or until cheese melts. Serve with orange and avocado slices.

North-of-the-Border Pozole

Makes about 6 servings

 A hearty Americanized version of the popular Mexican dish featuring hominy.

2 boneless skinless chicken breast halves, cut into strips	1 (4-oz.) can diced green chiles, drained
4 pork steaks, trimmed and cut into strips	½ teaspoon salt
1 (15-oz.) can hominy, drained	¼ teaspoon pepper
1 small onion, chopped	1 teaspoon chili powder
	Sliced radishes
	Chopped cilantro

Combine chicken, pork, hominy, onion, chiles, salt, pepper and chili powder. Cover and cook on LOW about 4 hours. Spoon into a serving bowl; sprinkle with sliced radishes and chopped cilantro.

Chinese Roast Chicken

Makes 4 to 6 servings

 Tastes as good cold as it does hot—try it in a chicken salad.

6 to 8 fresh parsley sprigs	1 (4- to 5-lb.) roasting chicken
1 celery stalk	1 tablespoon soy sauce
2 (2-inch) pieces gingerroot, peeled	2 teaspoons Chinese five spice
2 green onions	powder

Place a trivet or steamer basket in a slow cooker. Place parsley, celery, gingerroot and green onions inside roasting chicken. Tie chicken legs together with string. In a cup, mix soy sauce and Chinese five spice to make a paste. Spread mixture over chicken; place chicken, neck down, on trivet. Cover and cook on LOW 5 to 6 hours. Discard vegetables from inside chicken. Slice chicken to serve.

Chicken Tortilla Casserole

Makes 4 or 5 servings

This is a wonderful way to turn leftover chicken into a special meal in a dish. It fits nicely into the smaller slow cookers.

1 teaspoon dried oregano
¼ teaspoon garlic powder
1 (4-oz.) can chopped green chiles, drained
1 (8-oz.) can tomato sauce
6 corn tortillas
2 cups chopped cooked chicken
¾ cup shredded Monterey Jack cheese
3 tablespoons raw pumpkin seeds
Salsa

Grease a 6-cup baking dish that fits in slow cooker. In a small bowl, combine oregano, garlic powder, chiles and tomato sauce. Place 2 tortillas in bottom of greased baking dish. Layer 1 cup chicken over tortillas, ½ cup tomato mixture, ¼ cup cheese and 1 tablespoon pumpkin seeds. Tear 2 tortillas into bite-size pieces and spread over mixture. Repeat with remaining ingredients, ending with cheese and pumpkin seeds on top. Place baking dish in the slow cooker. Cover and cook on HIGH 4 to 5 hours. Serve with salsa.

Touch-of-the-Orient Chicken Rolls
Makes 6 servings

Individually wrapped servings of chicken make an unusual presentation on a bed of cooked rice.

¼ cup soy sauce
1 tablespoon sesame oil
¼ teaspoon dried red pepper flakes
1 tablespoon chopped chives
2 tablespoons chopped fresh cilantro
2 teaspoons grated gingerroot
1 (8-oz.) can sliced water chestnuts, drained
6 boneless skinless chicken breast halves
6 large lettuce leaves
3 tablespoons cornstarch
¼ cup water
1 (10-oz.) can mandarin oranges, drained

In a medium bowl, combine soy sauce, sesame oil, pepper flakes, chives, cilantro, gingerroot and water chestnuts; set aside. Wrap each chicken piece in a lettuce leaf; place in a slow cooker. Pour sauce with water chestnuts over chicken. Cover and cook on LOW 4 to 4½ hours or until chicken is tender. Remove chicken and cover to keep warm. Turn control to HIGH. In a small bowl, dissolve cornstarch in water; stir into sauce in cooker. Cover and cook on HIGH 15 to 20 minutes or until slightly thickened. Stir in oranges. To serve, spoon sauce over each serving.

Chicken Chop Suey

Makes 5 or 6 servings

No need to buy takeout chop suey—make this dish, bring out the chopsticks, and enjoy.

2 boneless skinless chicken breast halves
½ cup chopped celery
4 green onions, cut into 1-inch pieces
½ teaspoon salt
1 tablespoon chopped gingerroot
⅔ cup chicken broth
¼ cup soy sauce
½ teaspoon sugar
1 cup sliced fresh mushrooms
1 cup fresh bean sprouts
1 teaspoon sesame oil
2 tablespoons cornstarch
2 tablespoons water
Cooked rice

Cut chicken into strips about 1½ inches long and ¼ inch wide. Place in a slow cooker with celery, green onions, salt and gingerroot. In a small bowl, combine broth, soy sauce and sugar; pour mixture over chicken. Cover and cook on LOW 5 to 6 hours. Turn control to HIGH. Add mushrooms and bean sprouts. Cover and cook on HIGH about 5 minutes. Drizzle sesame oil over mixture; stir to mix. Dissolve cornstarch in water and stir into chicken mixture in cooker. Cover and cook on HIGH 10 to 15 minutes. Serve with cooked rice.

Curried Island Chicken

Makes 4 or 5 servings

 Let people choose their favorite combination of toppings.

1 (2½- to 3½-lb.) broiler-fryer chicken, cut up
1 (8-oz.) can pineapple chunks in juice
4 teaspoons curry powder
1 clove garlic, crushed
1 teaspoon chicken bouillon granules
1 tablespoon grated onion
½ teaspoon salt
⅛ teaspoon pepper
2 tablespoons cornstarch
2 tablespoons water
3 cups cooked rice
Shredded coconut, dates, raisins and/or chopped banana or papaya
Favorite chutney

Place chicken in a slow cooker. Drain pineapple and reserve juice and chunks separately. In a small bowl, combine reserved juice with curry powder, garlic, bouillon granules, onion, salt and pepper. Pour mixture over chicken. Cover and cook on LOW 4½ to 5 hours or until chicken is tender. Remove chicken from pot and keep warm. Turn control to HIGH. In a small bowl, dissolve cornstarch in water; stir cornstarch mixture and reserved pineapple chunks into slow cooker. Cover and cook on HIGH 15 to 20 minutes. Serve chicken and sauce over cooked rice. Sprinkle with your choice of accompaniments.

Mission Chicken

Makes 4 or 5 servings

 Seedless grapes and almonds add crunch to the slightly spicy orange sauce.

1 (2½- to 3½-lb.) broiler-fryer chicken, cut up
¼ teaspoon ground cinnamon
¼ teaspoon ground cloves
¼ teaspoon salt
½ teaspoon seasoned salt
¼ teaspoon lemon pepper
1 (6-oz.) can frozen orange juice concentrate, thawed
2 or 3 drops hot pepper sauce
3 tablespoons cornstarch
3 tablespoons water
1 cup seedless grapes, halved
¼ cup slivered toasted almonds (see Note, page 9)

Place chicken in a slow cooker. In a small bowl, combine cinnamon, cloves, salt, seasoned salt, lemon pepper, orange juice concentrate and hot pepper sauce. Pour mixture over chicken. Cover and cook on LOW about 5 hours or until chicken is tender. Turn control to HIGH. In a small bowl, dissolve cornstarch in water; stir into cooking juices in cooker. Cover and cook on HIGH 15 to 20 minutes or until thickened. Stir in grapes. Sprinkle with almonds.

Paella

Makes 6 to 8 servings

Saffron is the classic flavoring for this dish, but turmeric has been substituted for it here. If you have saffron, use a pinch in place of the turmeric.

4 chicken pieces, skinned
1 carrot, peeled and thinly sliced
½ onion, finely chopped
2 tomatoes, chopped
1 small smoked sausage, sliced (about 1 cup)
1 teaspoon turmeric
1 teaspoon dried oregano
3 cloves garlic, minced
¾ cup chicken broth
2 tablespoons chopped pimiento
¼ lb. shelled raw shrimp
6 to 8 small clams in shells or 1 (6½-oz.) can whole clams, drained
½ cup green peas
Salt and pepper to taste
2 cups cooked rice

In a slow cooker, combine chicken, carrot, onion, tomatoes, sausage, turmeric, oregano, garlic and chicken broth. Cover and cook on LOW 5 to 6 hours or until chicken is tender. Turn control to HIGH. Add pimiento, shrimp, clams and peas. Cover and cook on HIGH 30 minutes. Season with salt and pepper to taste. Stir in rice and serve.

Thai Chicken

Makes 8 servings

Turmeric turns this dish a beautiful golden color, and peanuts add crunchiness. Adjust the seasonings to suit your taste.

4 whole chicken breasts
1 tablespoon grated gingerroot
3 green onions, sliced
1 (14-oz.) can coconut milk
½ to ¾ teaspoon turmeric
¼ to ½ teaspoon dried red pepper flakes
1 (8-oz.) can pineapple chunks, drained
2 tablespoons cornstarch
2 tablespoons water
Cooked rice
½ cup chopped peanuts

Cut chicken breasts in half, making 8 pieces. Place chicken in a slow cooker. Add gingerroot, green onions, coconut milk, turmeric and pepper flakes. Cover and cook on LOW 4 to 5 hours or until chicken is tender. Turn control to HIGH; add pineapple. In a small bowl, dissolve cornstarch in water; stir into chicken mixture in cooker. Cover and cook on HIGH about 15 minutes. Serve over rice and sprinkle with peanuts.

Nostalgic Chicken & Herbed Dumplings

Makes 5 or 6 servings

 This dish is a time-honored favorite that's designed for today's busy families.

2 whole cloves
8 to 10 small white onions, halved
1 (2½- to 3½-lb.) broiler-fryer chicken, cut up
½ teaspoon salt
¼ teaspoon pepper
1 clove garlic, minced
½ teaspoon dried marjoram, crushed
½ teaspoon dried thyme, crushed
1 bay leaf
½ cup chicken broth
½ cup dry white wine
3 tablespoons cornstarch
¼ cup water
1 cup packaged biscuit mix
1 tablespoon chopped fresh parsley
6 tablespoons milk

Insert cloves in one onion. Place all onions in a slow cooker. Add chicken, salt, pepper, garlic, marjoram, thyme, bay leaf, broth and wine. Cover and cook on LOW 4 to 5 hours or until chicken is tender. Remove bay leaf and onion with cloves; discard. Turn control to HIGH. In a small bowl, dissolve cornstarch in water; stir into chicken mixture in cooker. Cover and cook while making dumplings; stir once. In a medium bowl, combine biscuit mix with parsley and milk, mixing with a fork until moistened. Drop by teaspoonfuls on chicken mixture around edges of pot. Cover and cook on HIGH 30 minutes or until dumplings are cooked in centers when tested with a fork.

Tarragon Chicken Thighs

Makes 8 servings

 Cooked chicken thighs are moist and juicy and rich with flavor.

½ teaspoon salt
⅛ teaspoon pepper
¼ cup margarine or butter, melted
1 tablespoon plus 1 teaspoon finely chopped fresh tarragon
8 chicken thighs
1 large tomato, peeled, seeded and chopped
1 green onion, chopped
¼ cup dry white wine
2 tablespoons cornstarch
½ cup half-and-half

In a medium bowl, combine salt, pepper, margarine or butter, and 1 tablespoon tarragon. Roll chicken pieces in melted butter mixture. Place in a slow cooker. Top with tomato, onion and wine. Cover and cook on LOW 5 to 6 hours. Remove chicken and cover to keep warm. Turn control to HIGH. In a small bowl, dissolve cornstarch in half-and-half; stir into cooking juices in cooker. Cover and cook on HIGH 20 minutes or until thickened. Add remaining teaspoon of fresh tarragon. Spoon sauce over chicken.

Red & Gold Sweet-Sour Chicken

Makes 4 to 6 servings

 You'll be proud to present this colorful dish on a bed of rice.

1 (2½- to 3½-lb.) broiler-fryer chicken, cut up
1 small onion, thinly sliced
1 cup chicken broth
¼ cup packed brown sugar
¼ cup vinegar
1 tablespoon hoisin sauce
½ teaspoon salt
⅓ cup cornstarch
⅓ cup water
1 red bell pepper, cut into chunks
1 mango, peeled and cut into chunks
½ cup jícama strips

Place chicken and onion in a slow cooker. In a small bowl, combine broth, brown sugar, vinegar, hoisin sauce and salt. Pour mixture over chicken. Cover and cook on LOW about 5 hours or until chicken is tender. Turn control to HIGH. In a small bowl, dissolve cornstarch in water; stir into chicken mixture in cooker. Add bell pepper. Cover and cook on HIGH 15 to 20 minutes. Stir in mango and jícama. Cover and cook 5 minutes.

Jambalaya

Makes 5 or 6 servings

If you enjoy spicy food, you can add some more heat to this Creole favorite with chiles or cayenne pepper after trying it as it is.

1 (2½- to 3½-lb.) broiler-fryer chicken, cut up
1 onion, chopped
½ cup finely chopped green bell pepper
1 carrot, peeled and thinly sliced
1 clove garlic, minced
1 teaspoon dried oregano
1 teaspoon dried basil
½ teaspoon salt
¼ teaspoon black pepper
¼ teaspoon paprika
¼ teaspoon dried red pepper flakes
1 (14-oz.) can tomatoes, cut up
1 lb. shelled raw shrimp
2 cups cooked rice

In a slow cooker, combine chicken, onion, bell pepper, carrot, garlic, oregano, basil, salt, black pepper, paprika, pepper flakes and tomatoes. Cover and cook on LOW 4 to 5 hours. Turn control to HIGH. Add shrimp and rice. Cover and cook on HIGH 30 to 40 minutes or until shrimp are pink.

Cornish Hens with Cherry Sauce

Makes 3 or 4 servings

Only three hens fit into a 3½-quart slow cooker; four fit into a 4- or 5-quart pot.

3 or 4 Cornish hens
1 (6-oz.) package Stove Top cornbread stuffing
1½ cups hot water
¼ cup plus 2 tablespoons margarine or butter
¾ cup red currant jelly
¼ cup pitted dried red cherries, coarsely chopped
2 teaspoons fresh lemon juice
½ teaspoon salt
¼ teaspoon ground allspice

Thaw hens if frozen. Place a rack in a slow cooker. In a medium bowl, combine stuffing mix with seasoning packet, water and ¼ cup of the margarine or butter. Stuff hens and place on rack in slow cooker. In a small saucepan, combine jelly, cherries, remaining 2 tablespoons margarine or butter, lemon juice, salt and allspice. Cook over LOW heat, stirring until jelly is melted. Reserve ⅔ cup sauce. Brush remaining sauce on hens in cooker. Cover and cook on LOW 6 to 7 hours. Serve whole or cut hens in half with kitchen shears. Spoon reserved sauce over hens at serving time.

Cornish Hens with Lime Glaze

Makes 4 servings

Here is the ideal entrée for an elegant meal. Serve with a fresh green vegetable and sliced tomatoes.

2 Cornish hens
2 slices cinnamon bread, cubed
1 celery stalk, chopped
½ teaspoon dried tarragon
2 tablespoons chopped walnuts
1 green onion, chopped
⅓ cup vermouth or white wine
3 tablespoons margarine or butter, melted
2 tablespoons sugar
2 tablespoons fresh lime juice
1 tablespoon soy sauce
3 tablespoons cornstarch
3 tablespoons water

Thaw hens if frozen. In a bowl, combine bread cubes, celery, tarragon, walnuts and green onion. Sprinkle with vermouth or white wine and toss. Spoon mixture into cavity of each hen. In a bowl, mix together margarine or butter, sugar, lime juice and soy sauce. Brush hens with sauce. Place a rack or trivet in a slow cooker. Place hens on end, neck down, on rack. Cover and cook on LOW 6 to 7 hours or until hens are tender. Remove hens and cover to keep warm. Turn control to HIGH. In a small bowl, dissolve cornstarch in water; stir into cooking juices. Cover and cook on HIGH 10 minutes or until thickened. With shears, cut hens in half. Spoon sauce over each.

Burgundy-basted Duckling

Makes 4 servings

For a golden brown duckling, place on broiler pan after cooking it in the slow cooker; then brown it in a 400F (205C) oven 15 to 20 minutes.

1 (4- to 5-lb.) ready-to-cook duckling
¼ cup Burgundy wine
1 tablespoon fresh lemon juice
½ teaspoon grated lemon peel
1 tablespoon Worcestershire sauce
1 clove garlic, minced
1 teaspoon salt
1 teaspoon dried marjoram, crushed
¼ teaspoon pepper
2 or 3 drops bottled hot pepper sauce

Place a rack in a 4-quart or larger slow cooker. With a fork, prick skin of duckling all over at approximately 2-inch intervals. Place duckling breast side down on rack in slow cooker. In a bowl, combine remaining ingredients. Brush half of wine mixture over duckling. Cover and cook on LOW 6 to 7 hours. If possible, remove fat with a bulb baster. Turn duckling and baste with more wine mixture once during cooking. Cut into serving pieces and serve hot.

Imperial Duckling

Makes 4 servings

A rosy sauce gives the duck a festive touch and delicious flavor.

1 (4- to 5-lb.) ready-to-cook duckling
2 tablespoons grated onion
¼ teaspoon dried tarragon
½ cup orange juice
⅛ teaspoon salt
⅛ teaspoon dry mustard
¼ cup currant jelly
2 tablespoons grated orange peel
2 tablespoons Port wine
2 teaspoons cornstarch
1 orange, peeled, sectioned and cut into chunks

Place a rack in a 4-quart or larger slow cooker. With a fork, prick skin of duckling all over at approximately 2-inch intervals. Place duckling on rack in slow cooker. (When cooking duckling in a 3½-quart (or smaller) slow cooker, cut the duckling into quarters or halves before putting it into the pot.) In a small saucepan, combine onion, tarragon, orange juice, salt, mustard, jelly, orange peel, wine and cornstarch. Cook over medium heat until thickened. Brush ⅓ cup sauce over duckling, reserving remaining sauce. Cover and cook on LOW 6 to 7 hours or until duckling is tender, turning once during cooking. If possible, remove fat with a bulb baster. Stir orange sections into remaining sauce, heat, and pour over duck just before serving.

Orange-Cranberry Turkey Fettuccine
Makes about 4 servings

A memorable main dish to serve during the holiday season or any time during the year.

1 lb. boneless skinless turkey breast and/or thighs
1 green onion, chopped
2 oranges, peeled and cut into small chunks
½ cup dried cranberries
½ cup orange juice
2 tablespoons brown sugar
1 tablespoon Worcestershire sauce
⅛ teaspoon freshly grated nutmeg
¼ teaspoon salt
⅛ teaspoon pepper
2 tablespoons cornstarch
3 tablespoons water
Cooked fettuccine
Chopped pecans

Cut turkey into thin strips. In a slow cooker, combine turkey with green onion, oranges, cranberries, orange juice, brown sugar, Worcestershire sauce, nutmeg, salt and pepper. Cover and cook on LOW about 4 hours or until turkey is tender. Turn control to HIGH. In a small bowl, dissolve cornstarch in water; stir into turkey mixture. Cover and cook on HIGH 15 to 20 minutes, stirring once. Serve over hot cooked fettuccine. Sprinkle with chopped pecans.

Stuffed Turkey Breast

Makes 8 or 9 servings

Prepare the stuffing first and the croutons will absorb all the delicious flavors while you prepare the turkey.

¼ cup margarine or butter, melted
1 small onion, finely chopped
1 celery stalk, finely chopped
2 cups herb-seasoned croutons (about 3½ oz.)
½ cup chicken broth
2 tablespoons minced fresh parsley
½ teaspoon poultry seasoning
1 whole uncooked turkey breast (about 5 lbs.)
Salt and pepper
½ cup dry white wine

Place a rack in a slow cooker. In a medium bowl, combine margarine or butter, onion, celery, croutons, broth, parsley and poultry seasoning. Slice turkey breast crosswise, from breastbone to ribcage, leaving slices attached to the bone. Sprinkle with salt and pepper.

Cut a piece of cheesecloth about 30 inches long. Soak cheesecloth in ¼ cup of the wine; place turkey on cheesecloth. Stuff bread mixture into slits of turkey. Fold cheesecloth over top of turkey. Place turkey on a rack in slow cooker. Pour remaining ¼ cup white wine over turkey. Cover and cook on LOW 7 to 8 hours or until tender. Remove turkey from cooker; discard cheesecloth. Serve each person one or more slices of turkey with dressing, plus some of the drippings.

Cran-Orange Turkey Roll

Makes 6 servings

None of your guests will suspect that this impressive dish is so simple to prepare.

¼ cup sugar
2 tablespoons cornstarch
¾ cup orange marmalade
1 cup fresh cranberries, ground or finely chopped
1 (2- to 2½-lb.) frozen turkey roll, partially thawed
Salt and pepper

In a small saucepan, blend sugar and cornstarch; stir in marmalade and cranberries. Cook and stir until mixture is bubbly and slightly thickened. Place turkey roll in a slow cooker. Sprinkle lightly with salt and pepper. Pour sauce over turkey. Cover and cook on LOW 9 to 10 hours. Insert a meat thermometer in turkey roll during the last 2 or 3 hours of cooking and cook until temperature reaches 185F (85C). Slice turkey roll. Spoon sauce over turkey slices.

Turkey with Leek & White Wine Sauce

Makes 4 to 6 servings

 If your favorite turkey parts are not available, substitute cut-up chicken.

2 leeks, trimmed and thinly sliced
2 teaspoons instant chicken bouillon granules
1 tablespoon margarine or butter, room temperature
⅓ cup finely chopped watercress
¼ teaspoon salt
⅛ teaspoon pepper
2 turkey thighs or 1 turkey breast half
¼ cup dry white wine
2 tablespoons cornstarch
½ cup nonfat sour cream

Place leeks in a slow cooker. Combine bouillon granules, margarine or butter, watercress, salt and pepper. Remove skin from turkey. Pat watercress mixture on all sides of turkey. Place turkey on top of leeks. Pour wine over turkey. Cover and cook on LOW 4½ to 5 hours or until turkey is tender. Remove turkey and keep warm. Turn control to HIGH. Stir cornstarch into sour cream and stir into cooking juices with leeks. Cover and cook on HIGH 10 to 15 minutes. Slice turkey; spoon leeks and sauce over turkey slices.

Turkey Fillets, Barbecue Style

Makes 6 or 7 servings

An easy way to prepare barbecued poultry, without worrying about lighting the charcoal and watching the fire.

6 or 7 boneless turkey fillets or cutlets
¼ cup molasses
¼ cup red wine vinegar
¼ cup ketchup
2 tablespoons Worcestershire sauce
½ teaspoon hickory smoke salt
1 tablespoon grated onion
½ teaspoon salt
⅛ teaspoon pepper
Cooked basmati or brown rice

Place turkey fillets in a slow cooker. In a small bowl, combine remaining ingredients except rice. Pour over turkey. Cover and cook on LOW about 4 hours. Serve with basmati or brown rice.

Southeast Asian-style Meatballs
Makes 8 to 10 meatballs

 Enjoy these main-dish meatballs or make them smaller for appetizers.

1 lb. uncooked ground turkey or lean pork
½ cup dry bread crumbs
1 egg, slightly beaten
2 tablespoons soy sauce
2 tablespoons hoisin sauce

2 teaspoons grated gingerroot
¼ teaspoon pepper
Plum Glaze (see below)
2 tablespoons toasted sesame seeds (see Note below)
Cooked noodles

PLUM GLAZE
½ cup plum jelly
1 tablespoon white wine vinegar

1 tablespoon ketchup
1 tablespoon sweet hot mustard

Place a rack in a slow cooker. In a medium bowl, combine ground turkey or pork, bread crumbs, egg, soy sauce, hoisin sauce, gingerroot and pepper. Form into 8 to 10 balls about 2 inches in diameter. Place on rack in slow cooker. If all meatballs don't fit in a single layer, poke small holes in 2 sheets of foil about 7 inches square. Cover bottom layer of meatballs with one sheet of foil; repeat with second layer of meatballs and another piece of foil. Cover and cook on LOW 3½ to 4 hours. Transfer to a serving dish. Prepare Plum Glaze and spoon over meatballs. Sprinkle with sesame seeds. Serve over cooked noodles.

Plum Glaze

Combine plum jelly, vinegar, ketchup and mustard. Stir over low heat or in microwave until smooth.

NOTE: Toast sesame seeds in a dry skillet over medium-low heat, stirring frequently, until golden brown. Nuts can be toasted the same way.

Turkey Lasagna

Makes 8 to 10 servings

 Turkey adds an exciting new flavor to lasagna, and a lower fat content.

1 lb. uncooked ground turkey
1 onion, chopped
1 clove garlic
1 (16-oz.) can peeled diced tomatoes in juice
1 (8-oz.) can tomato sauce
1 beef bouillon cube, crushed
1 tablespoon minced fresh parsley
2 teaspoons sugar
½ teaspoon salt
1 tablespoon chopped fresh basil
1 (15-oz.) container low-fat ricotta cheese
½ cup grated Parmesan cheese
1 teaspoon minced fresh oregano
8 oz. lasagna noodles, cooked and drained
8 oz. mozzarella cheese, thinly sliced

In a slow cooker, combine turkey, onion, garlic, tomatoes, tomato sauce, bouillon cube, parsley, sugar, salt and basil. Cover and cook on LOW 6 to 7 hours. In a medium bowl, mix ricotta cheese, ¼ cup of the Parmesan cheese and oregano.

Preheat oven to 350F (175C). In a 13 × 9-inch pan, layer half of the cooked noodles, sauce, mozzarella cheese and ricotta cheese mixture, and repeat, reserving enough sauce to layer on top. Sprinkle with remaining ¼ cup Parmesan cheese. Bake in preheated oven 45 minutes.

Short-Cut Turkey Chili

Makes 6 or 7 servings

Packaged ground turkey often has the skin ground in as a filler. For a lower-fat chili, have your butcher skin and grind the meat for you.

1 lb. uncooked ground turkey
1 onion, finely chopped
½ teaspoon salt
2 teaspoons chili powder
1 tablespoon Worcestershire sauce
1 (15-oz.) can tomato sauce
2 (16-oz.) cans kidney beans, drained

Thoroughly combine all ingredients in a slow cooker. Cover and cook on HIGH 3 to 4 hours or until onion is tender.

Ground Turkey Vegetable Round

Makes 6 to 8 servings

 Leftovers can be served cold or used for sandwiches.

1½ lbs. uncooked ground turkey
1 cup soft bread crumbs
⅓ cup pine nuts, toasted (see Note, page 9)
2 eggs, slightly beaten
¼ cup chopped green onions
1 tablespoon Dijon mustard
1 teaspoon prepared horseradish
1 tablespoon Worcestershire sauce
½ teaspoon salt
⅛ teaspoon pepper
1 medium zucchini
1 carrot, peeled

In a large bowl, combine turkey, bread crumbs, pine nuts, eggs, onions, mustard, horseradish, Worcestershire sauce, salt and pepper. In a food processor, shred zucchini and carrot. Stir vegetables into turkey mixture. Shape into a 6-inch ball. Place a metal rack in slow cooker. Place turkey round on 16-inch-long double thickness of cheesecloth. Gently lift into cooker and place on rack. Fold cheesecloth over meat. Cover and cook on LOW about 4½ hours. Lift out meat with ends of cheesecloth. Cut into 6 to 8 wedges. Spoon drippings over top.

Sausage Polenta Pie

Makes 5 or 6 servings

 A spicy mixture is hidden beneath a polenta topping.

1 (14-oz.) package reduced-fat smoked turkey sausage, cut into ½-inch slices
1 onion, finely chopped
1 clove garlic, crushed
1 tomato, peeled, seeded and chopped
1 (8-oz.) jar picante sauce
2 teaspoons chopped fresh basil
1 teaspoon chopped fresh oregano
1 tablespoon chopped fresh parsley
1 cup cornmeal
3¾ cups chicken broth
1 tablespoon margarine or butter
¼ cup grated Parmesan cheese

Combine sausage, onion, garlic, tomato, picante sauce, basil, oregano and parsley in a slow cooker; set aside. In a medium saucepan, combine cornmeal and broth. Bring to a boil; cook, stirring, over medium heat until thick, about 5 minutes. Stir in margarine or butter and half the cheese. Spoon on top of sausage mixture in slow cooker. Sprinkle with remaining cheese. Cover and cook on LOW about 6 hours. Serve with a large spoon directly onto plates.

Corn-stuffed Pork Chops, page 103; Stuffed Honeyed Sweet Potatoes, page 186; and steamed broccoli

Clockwise from top left: Calabacitas, page 191; Slow-Cooker Fajitas, page 64; Black Bean Chili with Pork, page 107; and Rio Grande Country Ribs, page 100

Clockwise from top left: Acorn Squash, Indonesian, page 188; Confetti Bean Casserole, page 162; and Sweet-Sour Bean Trio, page 166

Clockwise from top left: Carrot Coffee Cake, page 206; Stewed Pears with Ginger, page 225; and Apple-Cranberry Compote, page 233

Beans

Because slow cookers are newer electric cousins of the old-fashioned bean pot, bean dishes cook especially well in them. Today's cooks like to prepare beans in slow cookers because they can spend the day away from home while long, slow cooking is mingling compatible flavors to create traditional favorites or regional dishes.

Dried beans and peas are legumes, which include lentils, black-eyed peas, garbanzo or chickpeas, pinto beans, black beans, and many other types. Legumes are the richest source of vegetable protein and are a good source of soluble fiber. Nutritionists encourage us to increase our intake of legumes and grains because of their many benefits. In this chapter I offer Red Beans & Rice and Refried Black Beans, which highlight ethnic flavors from the South and West. Favorite Baked Beans and Fresh Black-eyed Peas add new zest to long-standing favorites.

You will notice that soaking is not called for in my recipes, but be sure to allow plenty of cooking time. Most bean recipes may be cooked longer than the times indicated or they may be cooked one day, refrigerated, and reheated for use the next day. Fiesta Turkey & Bean Salad is a two-day recipe that combines your slow-cooked beans with other ingredients in a hearty salad. For a vegetarian main dish, try Pizza Beans or Sour Cream Limas.

Most of the bean recipes serve six to eight people. You can double any of these recipes for a party if the quantity will fit in your slow cooker. While you are getting everything else ready, the beans cook with no fuss or bother. Then they stay hot until serving time in the slow cooker. In case you hadn't guessed—slow cookers are ideal buffet servers.

To make beans easier to digest, there are a number of over-the-counter commercial products available at your pharmacy. These are food enzymes which are meant to be sprinkled on cooked beans or taken in tablet form.

Red Beans & Rice

Makes 4 to 6 servings

 A slow-cooker version of a favorite traditional Southern dish.

1 lb. spicy smoked sausage, cut into ½-inch slices
2 (15-oz.) cans small red beans, drained
1 green or yellow bell pepper, chopped
1 jalapeño chile, seeded and finely chopped
1 (15-oz.) can peeled diced tomatoes in juice
1 small red onion, chopped
1 cup uncooked rice

In a slow cooker, combine sausage, beans, bell pepper, jalapeño chiles, tomatoes and onion. Cover and cook on LOW 5½ to 6 hours. Meanwhile, cook rice according to package directions. Spoon cooked rice into individual soup bowls or one large serving dish. Top with bean mixture.

Refried Black Beans

Makes 6 to 8 servings

These beans are an appetizing accompaniment to traditional pork roast as well as to enchiladas or tacos.

1 lb. dried black beans, rinsed
2 teaspoons chili powder
1 clove garlic, crushed
½ teaspoon ground cumin
1 small onion, chopped
½ teaspoon salt
6 cups water
1 tablespoon vegetable oil
4 oz. crumbled goat cheese (about ¾ cup)
2 tablespoons finely chopped fresh cilantro

In a slow cooker, combine beans, chili powder, garlic, cumin, onion, salt and water. Cover and cook on HIGH 6 to 7 hours or until beans are soft. Drain beans and partially mash with a potato masher or in a food processor, leaving about half of the beans whole. Just before serving, heat oil in a large skillet over medium heat. Add partially mashed beans, heat, and stir until fairly dry. Serve topped with goat cheese and cilantro.

Southwest Beef & Pintos

Makes about 8 servings

Just combine all the ingredients in the slow cooker. There's no overnight soaking, but remember that this dish takes almost twelve hours of cooking.

1 lb. dried pinto beans
4 cups beef broth
¼ lb. salt pork, sliced
1 lb. lean beef chuck steak, cut into 1-inch cubes
1 chopped red chile or ½ teaspoon crushed dried red pepper
1 medium onion, chopped
2 cloves garlic, minced
1 (6-oz.) can tomato paste
1½ tablespoons chili powder
1 teaspoon salt
1 teaspoon cumin seeds
½ teaspoon dried marjoram

Combine all ingredients in a slow cooker. Cover and cook on LOW 11 to 12 hours or until beans are tender.

Hot Sausage & Bean Stew
Makes 5 or 6 servings

 Leave this hearty main dish cooking while you are working or doing errands.

1 lb. dried pink beans
2 teaspoons chili powder
1 onion, chopped
1 yellow or orange bell pepper, chopped
1 clove garlic, crushed
2 tablespoons chopped cilantro
1 (15-oz.) can peeled diced tomatoes with juice
1 fresh jalapeño chile, seeded and chopped
3 cups hot water
¾ lb. spicy or hot bulk pork sausage

Combine all ingredients except sausage in a slow cooker. Meanwhile, lightly brown sausage in a medium skillet over medium heat; drain off fat. Add browned sausage to bean mixture. Cover and cook on LOW 8 or 9 hours or until beans are tender.

Fiesta Turkey & Bean Salad
Makes 6 to 8 servings

For an exciting main-dish salad, cook the beans a day ahead; cool and combine with other ingredients and refrigerate overnight.

1 cup dried kidney beans
1 cup dried garbanzo beans
¼ lb. smoked turkey, diced
5 cups water
2 tablespoons chopped fresh parsley
1 clove garlic, crushed
1 cup chopped cooked artichoke hearts or broccoli
1 small yellow or red bell pepper, chopped
½ cup olive oil
¼ cup white wine vinegar
2 tablespoons Dijon mustard
2 teaspoons honey
2 tablespoons chopped fresh chives
1 teaspoon dried dill weed
¼ teaspoon salt
⅛ teaspoon pepper
Lettuce
2 tablespoons watercress leaves

In a slow cooker, combine dried beans, turkey, water, parsley and garlic. Cover and cook on LOW 10 to 11 hours or until beans are tender but firm. Drain and discard liquid; cool drained bean mixture. Add artichokes or broccoli and bell pepper. In a medium bowl, combine oil, vinegar, mustard, honey, chives, dill weed, salt and pepper. Pour over bean mixture, cover and refrigerate. Line a serving bowl with lettuce; add bean mixture. Sprinkle with watercress.

Confetti Bean Casserole

Makes 5 or 6 servings

 Corn teams up with beans for a very popular hearty combination.

1 lb. dried small red or pinto beans
3½ cups chicken broth
½ lb. small smoked cocktail sausage links, halved
1 clove garlic, crushed
1 small onion, finely chopped
1 red or green bell pepper, chopped
2 tablespoons chopped fresh parsley
½ teaspoon salt
⅛ teaspoon pepper
1 cup cooked whole-kernel corn

Combine all ingredients except corn in a slow cooker. Cover and cook on LOW 6 to 7 hours or until beans are tender. Add corn about 30 minutes before turning off heat. Serve hot.

Favorite Baked Beans

Makes 6 to 8 servings

It is not necessary to soak beans ahead of time, but be sure to plan ahead and allow adequate cooking time.

1 lb. dried small white beans, rinsed
3½ cups water
⅓ cup molasses
¼ cup brown sugar
1 onion, chopped
¼ lb. salt pork, cut into 1-inch cubes
1 tablespoon prepared mustard
½ teaspoon salt

Combine all ingredients in a slow cooker. Cover and cook on HIGH 6 to 7 hours or until beans are tender.

Fresh Black-eyed Peas

Makes 4 to 6 servings

 Here's the perfect side dish to accompany broiled ham or chicken.

3 to 4 slices uncooked bacon, chopped
3 cloves garlic, crushed
4 green onions, tops included, finely chopped
1 cup chopped, peeled fresh or canned tomatoes
½ teaspoon salt
¼ teaspoon pepper
1 teaspoon dried oregano
1 cup water
1 lb. fresh or frozen black-eyed peas, thawed

Combine all ingredients in a slow cooker. Cover and cook on HIGH 5 to 6 hours.

Pizza Beans

Makes 6 to 8 servings

If possible, stir beans once or twice while they are cooking to ensure that they all are coated with sauce.

1 lb. dried great Northern beans
3½ cups water
4 tomatoes, peeled, seeded and chopped
1 onion, chopped
¼ cup chopped red or green bell pepper
1 clove garlic, crushed
1 teaspoon salt
½ teaspoon dried oregano, crushed
¼ teaspoon dried rosemary, crushed
1 cup (4 oz.) shredded mozzarella cheese
¼ cup grated Romano or Parmesan cheese

In a slow cooker, combine beans, water, tomatoes, onion, bell pepper, garlic, salt, oregano and rosemary. Cover and cook on HIGH 6 to 7 hours or until beans are tender. Top with mozzarella, then Romano cheese. Cover and cook another 10 minutes or until cheese melts.

Sweet-Sour Bean Trio

Makes 6 to 8 servings

A picnic wouldn't be complete without everyone's favorite bean salad. Serve hot or chilled.

4 bacon slices
1 onion, chopped
¼ cup packed brown sugar
1 teaspoon prepared mustard
1 clove garlic, crushed
1 teaspoon salt
¼ cup vinegar
1 (1-lb.) can lima beans, drained
1 (1-lb.) can baked beans, drained
1 (1-lb.) can kidney beans, drained

Cook bacon in a skillet until crisp; reserve drippings. Crumble bacon. Combine bacon and 2 tablespoons bacon drippings with onion, brown sugar, mustard, garlic, salt and vinegar. Combine mixture with beans in a slow cooker. Cover and cook on LOW 6 to 8 hours.

Sour Cream Limas

Makes 6 to 8 servings

It is important to stir beans after eight hours of cooking. This ensures a more even cooking of all the beans.

1 lb. dried baby lima beans
4 cups water
¼ cup margarine or butter, melted
½ cup brown sugar
¼ cup molasses
2 tablespoons prepared mustard
½ teaspoon salt
1 cup sour cream

Combine all ingredients except sour cream in a slow cooker. Cover and cook on LOW 8 hours. Stir beans; cover and continue cooking on LOW 3 to 4 hours or until beans are tender. Stir in sour cream.

Savory Tomato Limas
Makes 6 to 8 servings

 A hearty accompaniment to hot dogs or burgers.

1 lb. dried large lima beans, rinsed
3 cups water
1 onion, finely chopped
1 clove garlic, minced
1 tablespoon prepared mustard
1 tablespoon Worcestershire sauce
½ teaspoon salt
½ teaspoon chili powder
1 (10¾-oz.) can condensed tomato soup
2 tablespoons vinegar
2 tablespoons brown sugar
¼ lb. salt pork, cut into 1-inch cubes

Combine all ingredients in a slow cooker. Cover and cook on HIGH about 5 hours or until beans are tender.

Mac's Kidney Beans

Makes 8 to 10 servings

 Our friend Mac created a simple and thoroughly enjoyable recipe.

4 bacon slices, chopped
3 (15-oz.) cans kidney beans, drained
1 cup bottled chili sauce
½ cup sliced green onions
⅓ cup packed brown sugar

In a small skillet, cook bacon until crisp; reserve drippings. In a slow cooker, combine bacon and 2 tablespoons drippings with drained kidney beans, chili sauce and green onions. Sprinkle top with brown sugar. Cover and cook on LOW 4 to 6 hours. Keep beans hot and serve from cooker.

Slow-Cooker Cassoulet

Makes 5 or 6 servings

A French cassoulet is a hearty peasant dish featuring a country combination of beans with chicken or duck and sausage or other meats.

1 (2½- to 3½-lb.) broiler-fryer chicken, cut up
1 small leek, thinly sliced
1 clove garlic, crushed
3 tablespoons chopped fresh parsley
½ teaspoon salt
¼ teaspoon pepper
2 (15-oz.) cans white kidney beans, drained
½ lb. smoked sausage links, cut into ½-inch-thick slices
¼ cup dry white wine

In a slow cooker, combine chicken, leek, garlic, parsley, salt and pepper. Top with beans and sausage. Add wine. Cover and cook on LOW 5 to 6 hours or until chicken is tender.

Vegetables & Side Dishes

One of the greatest advantages of cooking vegetables in a slow cooker is being able to cook them ahead of time. It is not necessary to watch, stir or worry about boil-overs. You can be doing something else around the house or running errands. When you return, the vegetables are done. Serve them for dinner or combine them with other ingredients in a casserole that can be browned in the oven later and then served.

Rules for cooking vegetables vary almost as much as the vegetables themselves. For example, you will discover countless ways to prepare the squash family in your slow cooker. You can stuff acorn squash, mash banana squash and simmer zucchini. Herbed Squash Trio combines zucchini, crookneck and pattypan squash. Calabacitas is a spicy blend of zucchini, tomatoes, corn and chiles.

You can cook squash in your slow cooker, add other ingredients and finish the dish in the oven. When using squash in combination with other vegetables, cut the squash in large chunks, as they cook faster, in part due to a greater water content.

It is wise to turn the control to HIGH when you are cooking most vegetables in a slow cooker. Many of them have a tendency to dry out and discolor when left on LOW for a long time.

Dense vegetables like carrots, celery, turnips, parsnips, onions and beets take an extra-long time to cook in a slow cooker. Cut these kinds of vegetables into smaller pieces as suggested in the recipes for Carrots in Dilled Wine Sauce and Orange-Glazed Ginger Carrots. Strangely enough, these vegetables take as long or longer to cook than many meats. I suggest you thinly slice, chop, halve or quarter vegetables to ensure they get done in the specified cooking time. Be sure to consider this when combining vegetables with meat.

Recipes for sweet potatoes or yams may be interchanged. Use the one you prefer or whichever is available in your market. Sweet and white potatoes are delicious when "baked" in a slow cooker. Wash the potatoes but do not actually dry them. While still damp, place in the slow cooker and cook on LOW until soft and tender. Whole potatoes can be placed on top of a roast and will be done when the roast is. Try adding two or three potatoes to Dilled Pot Roast.

Rhineland Sweet-Sour Cabbage

Makes 5 or 6 servings

A popular accompaniment to spareribs or pork roast. In German families it's always served with Christmas dinner.

4 bacon slices, diced
¼ cup packed brown sugar
2 tablespoons all-purpose flour
½ teaspoon salt
⅛ teaspoon pepper
¼ cup water
¼ cup vinegar
1 medium head red cabbage, shredded (about 8 cups)
1 small onion, finely chopped

In a skillet, cook bacon until crisp; reserve drippings. Combine 1 tablespoon drippings in a slow cooker with remaining ingredients, except cooked bacon. Cover and cook on LOW 6½ to 7 hours or until cabbage is tender. Spoon into a serving bowl; sprinkle with reserved bacon.

Carrots in Dilled Wine Sauce

Makes 6 to 8 servings

Carrots are attractive and easy to eat when cut into ¼-inch sticks about 3 inches long.

8 medium carrots, peeled and cut into small sticks
½ cup chicken broth
½ cup dry white wine
1 teaspoon dried dill weed
3 tablespoons finely chopped shallots
½ teaspoon salt
1 tablespoon fresh lemon juice
2 tablespoons cornstarch
2 tablespoons water

Place carrots in a slow cooker. Combine broth, wine, dill weed, shallots, salt and lemon juice in a small bowl. Pour mixture over carrots. Cover and cook on HIGH 2 to 2½ hours or until carrots are tender. In a small bowl, dissolve cornstarch in water; stir into carrot mixture. Cover and cook on HIGH 10 to 15 minutes or until slightly thickened.

Orange-Glazed Ginger Carrots

Makes 5 or 6 servings

Try this dish on friends who claim they don't like vegetables, and watch them change their minds.

6 medium carrots, thinly sliced (about 3 cups)
3 tablespoons margarine or butter, melted
1 teaspoon grated gingerroot
3 tablespoons orange marmalade
2 tablespoons chopped pecans

Combine carrots, margarine or butter, gingerroot, marmalade and pecans in a slow cooker. Cover and cook on HIGH 2 to 3 hours or until carrots are tender.

Corn-Bacon Pudding

Makes 4 to 6 servings

A 4- or 5-cup metal mixing bowl makes a fine substitute for a mold or casserole dish.

4 bacon slices, cooked and crumbled
3 eggs, separated
1 (16-oz.) can whole-kernel corn, drained
1 cup evaporated skimmed milk
2 teaspoons sugar
1 tablespoon all-purpose flour
¼ teaspoon salt
¼ teaspoon pepper
¾ cup shredded Cheddar cheese
2 tablespoons chopped fresh parsley

Butter a 4- or 5-cup casserole dish or metal bowl that fits in your slow cooker. In a bowl, combine bacon, egg yolks, corn, milk, sugar, flour, salt and pepper. Stir in cheese. In a small bowl, beat egg whites until stiff but not dry. Fold egg whites and parsley into corn mixture. Spoon into prepared casserole dish. Cover top with foil, crimping edges to seal. Pour 2 cups hot water into a slow cooker and add a rack. Set casserole on rack in cooker. Cover and cook on LOW 4 to 5 hours or until a knife inserted off-center comes out clean. Serve warm directly from casserole dish with a large spoon.

Corn Stuffing Balls
Makes 8 servings

 Serve as an accompaniment to roast chicken or turkey, or grilled meats.

1 small onion, chopped
½ cup chopped celery with leaves
1 (17-oz.) can cream-style corn
¼ cup water
⅛ teaspoon pepper
1 teaspoon poultry seasoning
2 cups herb-seasoned stuffing mix (about 8 oz.)
2 eggs, slightly beaten
¼ cup margarine or butter, melted

In a bowl, combine onion, celery, corn, water, pepper, poultry seasoning, stuffing and eggs. Form into 8 balls. Place in bottom of a slow cooker; spoon margarine or butter over balls. Cover and cook on LOW 3½ to 4 hours.

Mock Chile Relleno

Makes 4 or 5 servings

How hot the chiles are will determine how spicy this flavorful Mexican combination is. Look for a "heat rating" on the side of the can.

2 (4-oz.) cans whole green chiles, drained
½ cup (2 oz.) shredded Cheddar cheese
1½ cups (6 oz.) shredded Monterey Jack cheese
1 (14½-oz.) can tomatoes, drained and sliced
3 eggs, separated
½ cup evaporated milk
1½ tablespoons all-purpose flour

Grease sides and bottom of a slow cooker. Remove seeds from chiles and cut into strips. Place half the chiles in the bottom of the cooker. Sprinkle with Cheddar cheese, then layer with remaining chiles, Jack cheese and tomatoes. Beat egg whites until stiff but not dry. Beat egg yolks slightly. Fold egg yolks and milk into egg whites. Fold in flour. Pour mixture over tomatoes. Cover and cook on HIGH 2 to 3 hours or until mixture is set. Serve while piping hot.

Eggplant-Artichoke Parmigiana

Makes 4 to 6 servings

 If you prefer, use homemade tomato sauce rather than canned.

1 medium eggplant
½ teaspoon salt
1 (14-oz.) jar tomato pasta sauce
1 (10-oz.) package frozen artichoke hearts, thawed and quartered
2 tablespoons capers, drained
2 teaspoons snipped fresh rosemary or ½ teaspoon dried
¼ teaspoon pepper
⅓ cup grated Parmesan cheese

Cut eggplant into ¾-inch slices. Cut slices in half; sprinkle with salt. Alternate layers of eggplant, pasta sauce, artichoke hearts and capers in a slow cooker. Sprinkle with rosemary and pepper. Cover and cook on HIGH 4 to 5 hours or until eggplant is tender. Sprinkle with cheese and serve.

Green Beans, Portuguese Style

Makes 8 servings

This recipe has received high praise for many years. Try it and you too will receive compliments.

¼ lb. salt pork
2 lbs. fresh green beans
2 medium tomatoes
2 cups beef bouillon
½ teaspoon salt
½ teaspoon sugar
¼ teaspoon pepper

Dice salt pork and spread over bottom of a slow cooker. Wash beans. Break each bean into 2 or 3 pieces; place in pot over salt pork. Peel, seed and cube tomatoes; spoon over beans. Add bouillon with salt, sugar and pepper. Cover and cook on HIGH 3 to 4 hours or until beans are tender. Drain and serve hot.

Leeks au Gratin

Makes 6 servings

Leeks are the mild members of the onion family; here they are combined with garlic and onion.

2 leeks
1 small onion, chopped
3 cloves garlic, chopped
1 celery stalk
1¼ cups chicken broth
½ teaspoon dry mustard
¼ cup cornstarch
½ cup evaporated milk
1 cup shredded Cheddar cheese
Salt and pepper to taste

Trim off tough green leaves from leeks. Cut leeks lengthwise and rinse to remove sand and dirt. Cut white part only into thin slices. Combine with onion, garlic, celery, broth and mustard in a slow cooker. Cook on LOW 6 to 7 hours. Turn control to HIGH. In a small bowl, dissolve cornstarch in milk; stir into leek mixture. Add cheese. Cover and cook on HIGH about 15 minutes until thickened and cheese has melted. Season with salt and pepper.

Sweet-Sour Baby Onions

Makes 6 servings

For a special treat, try these with grilled chicken or chops. Put them on about 4 hours before serving time and let them cook unattended.

2 (10-oz.) bags frozen small whole onions, thawed
2 tablespoons olive oil
2 tablespoons red wine vinegar
2 tablespoons brown sugar
1 teaspoon chicken bouillon granules or 1 bouillon cube
½ teaspoon salt
⅛ teaspoon pepper

In a bowl, combine onions and oil; toss until well coated. In a slow cooker, combine onions with vinegar, brown sugar, bouillon granules, salt and pepper. Cover and cook on LOW 4 to 4½ hours or until onions are soft.

Lemon Parsnips & Carrots

Makes 4 to 6 servings

Naturally sweet carrots and parsnips are enlivened with a refreshing lemon and mint sauce.

5 to 6 parsnips, peeled and thinly sliced (3 cups)
4 to 5 carrots, peeled and thinly sliced (3 cups)
2 cups chicken broth
¼ cup fresh lemon juice
3 tablespoons cornstarch
3 tablespoons water
2 tablespoons chopped fresh mint leaves

Place parsnips and carrots in a slow cooker. Pour in broth and lemon juice. Cover and cook on HIGH 2 to 4 hours or until vegetables are tender. In a small bowl, dissolve cornstarch in water; stir into vegetables with mint. Cover and cook 10 to 15 minutes.

Stuffed Green Peppers

Makes 5 servings

If all the peppers do not fit in the bottom of the slow cooker, carefully place three in one layer and two on top.

5 green bell peppers
½ lb. lean ground beef
¼ cup finely chopped onion
1 tablespoon chopped pimiento
½ teaspoon salt
1 (11- or 12-oz.) can whole-kernel corn, drained
1 tablespoon Worcestershire sauce
1 teaspoon prepared mustard
1 (10¾-oz.) can condensed tomato soup

Cut a slice off the top of each pepper. Remove core, seeds, and white membrane. In a bowl, combine beef, onion, pimiento, salt and corn. Spoon mixture into peppers. Stand peppers up in a slow cooker. Add Worcestershire sauce and mustard to undiluted soup; pour over peppers. Cover and cook on LOW 7 to 8 hours or until peppers are tender.

Herbed Squash Trio
Makes 6 to 8 servings

 This three-squash combination results in a colorful and appetizing vegetable dish.

4 zucchini (about 1¼ lbs.)
2 crookneck squash (about ½ lb.)
1 pattypan squash (about 2 oz.)
½ teaspoon salt
¼ teaspoon pepper
⅛ teaspoon garlic salt
¼ cup margarine or butter
¾ cup herb-seasoned croutons
3 tablespoons grated Parmesan cheese
1 tablespoon chopped fresh chives

Cut all the squash into ¾-inch pieces. Put squash in bottom of a slow cooker. Sprinkle with salt, pepper and garlic salt. Dot with margarine or butter. Sprinkle with croutons, then cheese and chives. Cover and cook on LOW 6 to 7 hours or until tender. Serve with a slotted spoon.

Stuffed Honeyed Sweet Potatoes

Makes 5 or 6 servings

 Cook and stuff the potatoes ahead of time, then heat in the oven at serving time.

5 to 6 sweet potatoes
½ cup margarine or butter, room temperature
¼ cup half-and-half
2 tablespoons honey
2 tablespoons dark rum
½ teaspoon ground cardamom
¼ teaspoon salt
2 tablespoons chopped walnuts

Wash potatoes; place damp potatoes in a slow cooker. Cover and cook on LOW about 5 hours or until done. Cut off top third of each potato lengthwise and scoop out interior, leaving a ¼-inch shell. Mash potato pulp with margarine or butter, half-and-half, honey, rum, cardamom and salt. Return mixture to shells. Top with walnuts.

Arrange potatoes on a shallow baking sheet. Preheat oven to 425F (220C) if serving now or cover and refrigerate to serve later. Bake 15 minutes or until hot and lightly browned.

Stuffed Potatoes

Makes 5 or 6 servings

Be creative and add additional toppings such as chopped pimiento, salsa, nuts or herbs.

5 to 6 large baking potatoes
3 tablespoons margarine or butter
½ cup milk
½ cup sour cream
1 teaspoon salt
⅛ teaspoon pepper
2 tablespoons grated Parmesan cheese
Chopped fresh chives

Wash potatoes; drain but do not dry. Place damp potatoes in a slow cooker. Cover and cook on LOW 6 to 8 hours or until tender. Remove from cooker. Cut off top third of each potato lengthwise and scoop out interior, leaving a ¼-inch shell. Mash potato pulp. Add margarine or butter, milk, sour cream, salt and pepper. Beat until fluffy, adding more milk if necessary. Spoon mixture into shells, mounding tops. Sprinkle with cheese.

Place potatoes in a shallow baking pan. Preheat oven to 425F (220C) if serving now or cover and refrigerate to serve later. Bake 15 minutes or until hot and lightly browned. Top with chopped chives.

Acorn Squash, Indonesian

Makes 6 servings

Choose your favorite chutney or try Fresh Mango Chutney (page 222) or Nectarine Chutney (see page 221).

3 acorn squash
Salt and pepper
¼ cup margarine or butter, melted
⅓ cup chutney
⅓ cup flaked coconut

Cut each squash in half; remove seeds. Wash and drain excess water but do not dry. Sprinkle with salt and pepper. Place in a slow cooker. Cover and cook on LOW 3 to 5 hours or until tender. Remove from cooker and place cut side up on a broiler pan or heatproof platter.

Preheat oven to 400F (205C). Brush inside of squash with margarine or butter. Mix chutney and coconut; spoon mixture into cavities of squash. Bake about 15 minutes or until bubbly.

Potato & Turnip Whip

Makes 6 servings

The texture of this dish is better if the vegetables are cooked on HIGH, then drained and mashed.

4 turnips, peeled and quartered (about 20 oz.)
4 medium potatoes, peeled and quartered (about 24 oz.)
¼ cup chopped onion
5 to 6 cups water
¼ cup half-and-half
2 tablespoons margarine or butter, room temperature
½ teaspoon salt
⅛ teaspoon pepper

In a slow cooker, combine turnips, potatoes and onion. Cover with water. Cover and cook on HIGH about 4 hours or until vegetables are tender. Drain well. Mash vegetables; add half-and-half, margarine or butter, salt and pepper. Beat until fluffy.

Old-Fashioned Stewed Tomatoes

Makes 5 or 6 servings

Seasoned croutons top off this dish, which has been a family favorite for several generations.

4 to 5 large ripe tomatoes
2 tablespoons margarine or butter
1 onion, thinly sliced
½ cup chopped celery
¼ cup chopped green bell pepper
½ teaspoon sugar
1 tablespoon chopped fresh basil
1 tablespoon chopped fresh parsley
1 bay leaf
½ teaspoon salt
⅛ teaspoon pepper
1 cup seasoned croutons

Dip tomatoes in boiling water 20 to 30 seconds. Drop into cold water and remove skins. Halve tomatoes, remove seeds and core. Coarsely chop tomatoes.

Combine tomatoes in a slow cooker with margarine or butter, onion, celery, bell pepper, sugar, basil, parsley, bay leaf, salt and pepper. Cover and cook on LOW 6 to 7 hours. Remove bay leaf and discard. Top with croutons.

Calabacitas

Makes 5 or 6 servings

A versatile side dish by itself, or add cooked beans and use as a filling for vegetarian tacos or enchiladas.

2 medium zucchini
1 (16-oz.) can stewed tomatoes with juice
1 small onion, chopped
1 cup cooked whole-kernel corn
1 (4-oz.) can roasted green chiles, chopped
1 teaspoon dried oregano
½ teaspoon sugar
Salt and pepper

Cut zucchini into ¾-inch pieces. Combine all ingredients in a slow cooker. Cover and cook on HIGH 2 to 3 hours or until zucchini is tender. Season with salt and pepper to taste.

Creole Zucchini

Makes 6 or 7 servings

 Fortunately these ingredients are available year round.

2 lbs. zucchini
1 small green bell pepper, chopped
1 small onion, chopped
1 clove garlic, minced
1 teaspoon salt
¼ teaspoon pepper
4 tomatoes, peeled and chopped
2 tablespoons margarine or butter
2 tablespoons minced fresh parsley

Cut zucchini into ¼-inch slices. In a slow cooker, combine zucchini, bell pepper, onion, garlic, salt and pepper. Top with chopped tomatoes, then margarine or butter. Cover and cook on HIGH about 2 hours or until zucchini is tender. Sprinkle with chopped parsley.

Curried Barley

Makes 8 servings

Enjoy a tasty side dish that's high in fiber and delicious paired with grilled chicken.

    4 cups chicken broth
    ⅔ cup barley
    1 to 2 carrots, peeled and chopped
    2 garlic cloves, minced
    ¼ teaspoon red (cayenne) pepper
    ½ teaspoon curry powder
    ½ cup raisins or dried currants
    ½ cup chopped onions
    Plain yogurt

Combine all ingredients except yogurt in a slow cooker. Cover and cook on HIGH 3 to 4 hours or until all liquid is absorbed and vegetables are tender. Serve topped with yogurt.

Orange Barley Casserole
Makes 6 to 8 servings

 Here's an especially tasty accompaniment for broiled ham slices.

2 cups orange juice
⅓ cup barley
¼ cup dried currants
¼ cup dried apricots, halved
¼ cup chopped dates

1 apple, peeled, cored and chopped
½ teaspoon ground allspice
2 to 3 tablespoons chopped
walnuts or pecans

In a slow cooker, combine all ingredients. Cover and cook on LOW 3 to 4 hours. Serve warm.

Lentil Casserole
Makes 6 to 8 servings

A nutritious side dish that can become a main-dish salad by adding chopped cucumber and lettuce.

1 cup lentils
2 bacon slices, chopped
1 cup stewed tomatoes, chopped, with
    juice
1 teaspoon Chinese five spice powder

¼ teaspoon dried red pepper flakes
1 small onion, chopped
1 cup water

Rinse lentils; pick out any debris. Place all ingredients in a slow cooker. Cover and cook on LOW 7 to 8 hours or until all liquid is absorbed. Serve hot or cold.

Couscous Provençal

Makes 5 or 6 servings

If using canned tomatoes, increase couscous to ½ cup. Enjoy this side dish hot or chilled.

3 cups peeled chopped fresh tomatoes or 1 (14-oz.) can tomatoes
3 green onions, chopped
4 cloves garlic, crushed
½ teaspoon dried thyme
1 teaspoon dried basil
⅓ cup couscous
½ cup ripe olives, sliced
Feta or blue cheese

In a slow cooker, combine tomatoes, green onions, garlic, thyme and basil. Cover and cook on LOW 5 to 6 hours. Stir in couscous and olives. Turn control to HIGH. Cover and cook on HIGH 25 to 30 minutes. Serve sprinkled with crumbled cheese.

Shades of Autumn Rice

Makes 4 to 6 servings

A combination of popular fall flavors enhances rice in the slow cooker—an ideal accompaniment to roast pork or chicken.

1 cup uncooked brown rice
1½ cups apple juice or cider
1 (10½-oz.) can condensed chicken broth
1 apple, peeled, cored and chopped
⅓ cup golden raisins
¼ cup chopped walnuts
1 tablespoon brown sugar
¼ teaspoon freshly grated nutmeg
½ teaspoon ground cinnamon
½ teaspoon salt

Combine all ingredients in a slow cooker. Cover and cook on LOW 4 to 5 hours or until rice is tender.

Marinara Sauce

Makes about 3 cups

For an Italian-style seafood sauce, add 1 pound cooked shrimp, clams or scallops at the end and cook on HIGH 10 to 15 minutes.

1 (16-oz.) can peeled tomatoes, cut up
1 (6-oz.) can tomato paste
1 clove garlic, minced
2 tablespoons minced fresh parsley
1 teaspoon dried oregano
½ teaspoon dried basil
1 teaspoon salt
¼ teaspoon pepper
½ teaspoon seasoned salt
Cooked spaghetti
Grated Parmesan cheese

In a slow cooker, combine tomatoes, tomato paste, garlic, parsley, oregano, basil, salt, pepper and seasoned salt. Cover and cook on LOW 6 to 7 hours. Serve over cooked spaghetti. Top with Parmesan cheese.

Vegetarian Sauce

Makes 6 to 8 servings

 Use this tasty sauce as a topping for pasta or rice, or spoon over an omelet.

⅓ cup dried mushrooms, rinsed
6 sun-dried tomatoes, cut in halves
1 (28-oz.) can crushed tomatoes
½ medium onion, finely chopped
2 cloves garlic, crushed
1 (15-oz.) can white kidney beans (cannellini), drained
½ cup red wine
2 tablespoons chopped green bell pepper
⅓ cup green peas, fresh or frozen and thawed
1 tablespoon chopped fresh parsley
Salt and pepper
Cooked pasta or rice
Crumbled goat or blue cheese

Break dried mushrooms in pieces; discard tough stems. In a slow cooker, combine mushrooms with sun-dried tomatoes, crushed tomatoes, onion, garlic, beans, wine and bell pepper. Cover and cook on HIGH 2½ to 3½ hours. Add peas and parsley. Cover and cook 15 minutes. Season with salt and pepper to taste. Serve over pasta or rice; sprinkle with crumbled goat or blue cheese.

Breads & Cakes

Steamed breads and "puddings," such as Banana Nut Bread and Persimmon Pudding, are moist and delicious when made in your slow cooker. An old holiday favorite from England, Traditional Plum Pudding is filled with dried fruits and nuts. With the even temperature in your slow cooker, you don't need to constantly check for water or worry about cakes and breads drying out on the surface.

There are a few tricks to remember when "baking" in one of these pots. First, turn the control to HIGH. The LOW setting is too low to give breads and cakes the texture you expect. With breads and cakes, you will need an additional container inside the slow cooker, covered with a lid or foil. The container is placed on a metal rack or trivet inside the pot. If you don't have a metal rack or trivet to fit your slow cooker, crumple foil and place it in the bottom of the cooker to support the baking container. Pour 2 cups of hot water around the container to provide steam for cooking the bread.

As a rule, it is not a good idea to remove the lid or foil from the bread container during the first 2 hours of cooking. After that, check the bread by inserting a wooden pick in the mixture. If the pick comes out clean, the bread is done.

For some recipes, such as Blueberry Coffee Cake and Cornbread, the procedure is slightly different. Cakes are "baked" in a pan set directly on the bottom of the slow cooker, similar to the way you would do it in an oven. It is not necessary to use a trivet or water. Instead of covering the uncooked cake mixture with foil or a lid, cover the top with four or five layers of paper towels. Because there is more moisture in a slow cooker than in an oven, it is necessary to compensate for this with the paper towels to help absorb the moisture on top of the cake. Also, leave the lid of your slow cooker slightly open to let extra moisture escape.

The type and kind of container to use for breads and cakes will depend on the size of your pot. In addition to molds and coffee cans, metal mixing bowls, springform or small Bundt pans make excellent containers. The following containers hold approximately the same amount of batter so you can substitute one for another:

1 (2-lb.) coffee can	1 (1½-quart) baking dish
1 (6- or 7-cup) mold	3 (16-oz.) vegetable cans
2 (1-lb.) coffee cans	

Traditional Plum Pudding

Makes 6 to 8 servings

Celebrate the holiday season in grand style by presenting this triumph at the end of dinner.

4 slices bread, torn into pieces
1 cup milk
2 eggs
1 cup packed brown sugar
¼ cup orange juice
1 teaspoon vanilla extract
½ cup finely chopped or ground suet or vegetable shortening
1 cup all-purpose flour
1 teaspoon baking soda
½ teaspoon salt
2 teaspoons ground cinnamon
1 teaspoon ground cloves
1 teaspoon ground mace
2 cups raisins
1 cup chopped pitted dates
½ cup chopped mixed candied fruits and peels
½ cup coarsely chopped walnuts

Place a metal rack or trivet in a slow cooker. Grease a 2-quart mold; set aside. In a medium bowl, soak bread in milk 10 minutes. Beat in eggs, sugar, juice and vanilla. Stir in suet or shortening. In a large bowl, combine flour, soda, salt and spices. Add raisins, dates, candied fruit and peels, and walnuts, and mix well. Add bread mixture. Pour into prepared mold. Cover with foil. Add 1 inch hot water to slow cooker. Place mold on rack in slow cooker. Cover and cook on HIGH 5 to 6 hours. Remove from slow cooker; cool in pan 10 minutes. Loosen pudding from sides of mold with a small spatula. Invert on plate to unmold. Serve warm, plain or with Brandy Hard Sauce (page 212).

Persimmon Pudding

Makes 6 to 8 servings

The bright orange, fig- or heart-shaped Hachiya persimmon should be very soft. The reddish-orange, tomato-shaped Fuyu can be slightly firm.

1½ cups all-purpose flour
1 cup sugar
1 teaspoon baking powder
1 teaspoon baking soda
1 teaspoon ground cinnamon
¼ teaspoon freshly grated nutmeg
2 persimmons
1 tablespoon fresh lemon juice
⅓ cup milk
1 egg
2 tablespoons maple syrup
¼ cup margarine or butter, melted
½ cup chopped dried apricots
¼ cup chopped pistachios

HOT LIME SAUCE
2 tablespoons cornstarch
½ cup sugar
½ cup water
½ cup fresh lime juice
2 tablespoons margarine or butter
¼ teaspoon grated lime peel
3 tablespoons fresh lemon juice

Place a metal rack or trivet in a slow cooker. Grease a 6- or 8-cup heatproof mold. In a large bowl, combine flour, sugar, baking powder, soda, cinnamon and nutmeg; set aside. Cut persimmons in half; scoop out pulp. Process lemon juice and pulp in a blender or food processor until pureed. Add milk, egg, maple syrup, and margarine or butter; process until well blended. Stir liquid into flour mixture. Add apricots and pistachios. Spoon into prepared mold; cover with foil. Place on rack in slow cooker. Pour in boiling water until it comes halfway up the sides of the mold. Cover and steam on HIGH 3 hours. Remove mold from cooker. Loosen sides by inserting a thin knife between pudding and sides of mold. Invert on a platter. Prepare Hot Lime Sauce. Serve pudding warm with sauce.

Hot Lime Sauce

Makes about 1¹/₂ cups

In a small saucepan, combine cornstarch and sugar. Add water and lime juice, and stir until smooth. Cook, stirring, over medium-low heat until thickened and translucent. Add margarine or butter; stir until melted. Remove from heat. Stir in lime peel and lemon juice.

Chocolate Pudding Cake
Makes 6 to 8 servings

Chocolate sauce gives an even richer flavor to this chocolate lovers' fantasy come true.

2 cups all-purpose flour
2 teaspoons baking powder
¼ teaspoon salt
½ cup unsweetened cocoa powder
½ cup margarine or butter, room temperature
½ cup sugar
4 eggs
1 cup milk
1½ cups fresh bread crumbs
Chocolate or fudge sauce
Whipped cream (optional)

Place a metal rack or trivet in a slow cooker. Grease a 1½-quart mold or baking dish. Sift flour, baking powder, salt and cocoa into a bowl. In a large bowl, cream margarine or butter and sugar. Add eggs, one at a time, alternately with half the flour mixture, beating well after each addition. Add milk alternately with remaining flour. Stir in bread crumbs. Pour into prepared mold and cover with foil. Add 2 cups hot water to slow cooker. Place mold with cake mixture on rack in cooker. Cover and cook on HIGH 3 to 4 hours. Serve warm or cold. To serve, slice cake and top each serving with chocolate or fudge sauce and whipped cream, if desired.

Blueberry Coffee Cake

Makes 4 to 6 servings

This dense blueberry coffee cake tastes great and would be ideal for Sunday brunch.

1 cup all-purpose flour
½ cup sugar
2 teaspoons baking powder
¼ teaspoon salt
1 egg, beaten
¼ cup vegetable oil
2 tablespoons milk
½ teaspoon vanilla extract
1 cup fresh or thawed frozen blueberries, drained
Cinnamon sugar or powdered sugar

Grease a 1½-quart mold or baking dish. In a bowl, combine flour, sugar, baking powder and salt. Add egg, oil, milk and vanilla; beat until smooth. Fold in blueberries. Pour into prepared mold. Place in a slow cooker. Cover mold with 4 or 5 paper towels. Cover and cook on HIGH 3 to 4 hours. Cool on rack 5 minutes. Remove from mold and sprinkle with cinnamon sugar or powdered sugar. Serve warm.

Carrot Coffee Cake

Makes 4 to 6 servings

Not quite as sweet or rich as traditional carrot cake, this version is just right for brunch. For special occasions, drizzle with powdered-sugar frosting.

2 eggs
¾ cup sugar
⅓ cup vegetable oil
1½ cups all-purpose flour
1 teaspoon baking powder
½ teaspoon baking soda
⅛ teaspoon salt
1 teaspoon ground cinnamon
1 cup grated carrot (2 medium)

Place a metal rack or trivet in a slow cooker. Grease and flour a 6-cup mold. In a large bowl, beat eggs. Add sugar gradually, beating until slightly thickened. Add oil gradually and continue beating until thoroughly combined. Stir dry ingredients together and stir into liquid mixture until smooth. Stir in carrots. Pour into prepared mold. Cover with foil. Pour 2 cups hot water into slow cooker. Place covered mold on rack. Cover and cook on HIGH about 3½ hours or until firm. Remove from slow cooker. Let stand at room temperature 10 minutes. Loosen cake from sides of mold with a small spatula. Invert onto cooling rack. Cut into thin wedges to serve.

Banana Nut Bread

Makes about 6 servings

A great way to use ripe bananas. Serve slices of this bread plain, or spread with peanut butter, cream cheese or marmalade.

⅓ cup vegetable shortening
½ cup sugar
2 eggs
1¾ cups all-purpose flour
1 teaspoon baking powder
½ teaspoon baking soda
½ teaspoon salt
1 cup mashed ripe bananas (2 medium)
½ cup chopped walnuts

Place a metal rack or trivet in a slow cooker. Grease a 5- or 6-cup mold; set aside. Cream shortening and sugar in a large bowl. Add eggs and beat well. Combine dry ingredients; add to creamed mixture alternately with mashed banana, blending well after each addition. Stir in nuts. Pour into prepared mold. Cover mold with foil. Add 2 cups hot water to slow cooker. Place mold on rack in cooker. Cover and cook on HIGH about 3 hours or until bread is firm. Remove from cooker. Let stand 10 minutes in mold. Loosen edges with a small spatula; invert on plate. Slice and serve warm.

Blueberry & Orange Bread

Makes 6 servings

Begin with a mix and make it doubly good with two types of blueberries, accented with orange.

1 (14-oz.) package blueberry muffin mix
½ cup orange juice
1 egg
⅓ cup dried blueberries
⅓ cup chopped walnuts
1 tablespoon grated orange peel

Grease a 5- to 6-cup mold or baking dish. Drain canned blueberries from mix in a strainer; set aside. Pour mix into a large bowl. Stir in orange juice and egg. Mix to combine; fold in drained blueberries, dried blueberries, walnuts and orange peel. Spoon mixture into greased mold. Place mold in a slow cooker. Cover mold with 2 to 3 pieces of paper towel. Cover and cook on HIGH 2½ to 3 hours. Remove from pot and let stand 20 minutes. Invert mold onto a serving dish; let cool before slicing.

VARIATION: If using a mix with dried rather than canned blueberries, add to mixture with walnuts and orange peel.

Cornbread

Makes 4 to 6 servings

 A tasty moist bread to serve with beans and a green salad.

1 cup cornmeal
1 cup all-purpose flour
2 tablespoons sugar
1 tablespoon baking powder
½ teaspoon chili powder
1 egg
3 tablespoons vegetable oil
1 cup milk

Grease a 6- to 7-cup baking dish. In a bowl, stir all dry ingredients together. In a small bowl, beat together egg, oil and milk. Pour liquid ingredients into cornmeal mixture and stir to combine. Pour batter into prepared baking dish. Place dish in bottom of slow cooker. Cover with 2 to 3 pieces paper towel. Cover and cook on HIGH 4½ to 5 hours or until firm. Serve warm.

Steamed Molasses Bread

Makes 6 servings

Cut warm bread into slices or thin wedges and spread with plain or orange-flavored butter.

2 cups All-Bran cereal
2 cups whole-wheat flour
2 teaspoons baking powder
1 teaspoon baking soda
½ teaspoon salt
1 cup raisins
1 egg
1¾ cups buttermilk
½ cup molasses

Place a metal rack or trivet in a slow cooker. Grease and flour an 8-cup mold; set aside. In a medium bowl, combine cereal, flour, baking powder, soda, salt and raisins. In a large bowl, beat egg. Add milk and molasses, and stir to combine. Stir in dry ingredients; do not overbeat. Pour into prepared mold. Cover with foil. Pour 2 cups hot water into slow cooker. Place covered mold on rack. Cover slow cooker and cook on HIGH 3½ to 4 hours. Remove mold from pot. Let stand 5 minutes. Loosen edges with small spatula, then invert on plate. Serve warm.

Peanut Butter Bread
Makes 6 servings

 All-American flavors that have been favorites for many generations.

¾ cup hot water
¾ cup peanut butter
¾ cup milk
⅓ cup sugar
¼ teaspoon salt
1 egg, slightly beaten
2 cups all-purpose flour
4 teaspoons baking powder
¾ cup chopped salted peanuts

Place a metal rack or trivet in a slow cooker. Grease a 5- or 6-cup mold. In a large bowl, pour hot water over peanut butter. Stir in milk, sugar, salt, egg, flour, baking powder and peanuts. Stir well. Spoon batter into prepared mold. Cover with foil. Pour 2 cups hot water into slow cooker. Place mold on rack. Cover and cook on HIGH about 5 hours. Remove mold and let stand 10 minutes. Turn out on cooling rack. Slice and serve warm or cool. Spread with butter, marmalade or jam.

Tropical Bread with Brandy Hard Sauce
Makes 6 servings

Fragrant fresh mangoes are combined with other tropical flavors to create an exciting dessert.

1 cup mango pulp

¾ cup orange juice

1 egg, beaten

¼ cup chopped dried persimmon
 or papaya

½ cup dried banana chips

½ cup pine nuts or pecans

¼ cup golden raisins

2 cups all-purpose flour

2 teaspoons baking soda

½ cup sugar

1 tablespoon margarine or butter,
 melted

½ teaspoon vanilla extract

BRANDY HARD SAUCE

2 cups powdered sugar

½ cup butter, room temperature

2 to 3 tablespoons brandy or
 brandy extract to taste

Place a metal rack or trivet in a slow cooker. Grease a 6-cup baking dish or mold. In a large bowl, beat together mango pulp, orange juice and egg. Stir in and thoroughly combine remaining ingredients. Pour into prepared baking dish or mold; set on rack in slow cooker. Add 1½ cups water to slow cooker. Cover and cook on HIGH 3 to 3½ hours. Remove mold from slow cooker; let stand 20 minutes. Invert onto serving dish. Prepare Brandy Hard Sauce. Serve warm or cold with hard sauce.

Brandy Hard Sauce
Makes about 1¹/₄ cups

In a small bowl, combine sugar, butter and brandy extract. Mix until smooth and thoroughly combined.

Blueberry Brown Bread
Makes 6 servings

Dried blueberries and cherries are available in many supermarkets and gourmet stores. They contribute a welcome flavor without additional liquid.

1 cup cornmeal
1 cup rye flour
1 cup whole-wheat flour
1½ teaspoons baking soda
½ teaspoon salt
½ cup dried blueberries or cherries
¾ cup molasses
2 cups buttermilk

Place a metal rack or trivet in a slow cooker. Grease an 8-cup mold. In a large bowl, combine cornmeal, rye flour, whole-wheat flour, baking soda, salt, and dried blueberries or cherries. Add molasses and buttermilk, stirring just until blended. Spoon into prepared mold. Cover with foil. Add 2 cups hot water to slow cooker. Place mold on rack. Cover and cook on HIGH 3 to 3½ hours. Remove mold from cooker. Let stand on cooling rack 5 to 10 minutes. Unmold; slice and serve warm.

NOTE: To make a buttermilk substitute, add 1 tablespoon lemon juice for each cup of milk or follow the instructions on package of dry buttermilk mix.

Pumpkin Nut Bread

Makes 6 to 8 servings

Make this unusual bread when you have canned pumpkin left over from the holidays, or any time during the year.

1½ cups all-purpose flour
1¼ teaspoons baking soda
½ teaspoon salt
1 teaspoon ground cinnamon
½ teaspoon freshly grated nutmeg
1 cup canned pumpkin
1 cup sugar
½ cup buttermilk
1 egg
2 tablespoons margarine or butter, room temperature
1 cup chopped pecans

Place a metal rack or trivet in a slow cooker. Grease and flour a 5- to 6-cup mold. In a large bowl, combine all ingredients except pecans and beat until well blended. Stir in nuts. Spoon into prepared mold. Cover with foil. Pour 2 cups hot water in cooker. Place covered mold on rack. Cover and cook on HIGH 3½ to 4 hours. Turn out on cooling rack. Serve warm or cool.

Date & Nut Loaf
Makes 6 servings

Our favorite bread. For added goodness, spread thinly sliced bread with butter, cream cheese or peanut butter.

1 cup boiling water
1 cup chopped dates
¾ cup sugar
1 egg, slightly beaten
1½ teaspoons baking soda
¼ teaspoon salt
1 teaspoon vanilla extract
1 tablespoon vegetable oil
1½ cups all-purpose flour
½ cup walnuts, chopped

Place a metal rack or trivet in a slow cooker. Grease a 6-cup mold. In a large bowl, pour boiling water over dates. Let stand 5 to 10 minutes. Stir in sugar, egg, baking soda, salt, vanilla, oil, flour and walnuts. Pour into prepared mold. Cover with foil. Pour 2 cups hot water into slow cooker. Place filled and covered mold on rack. Cover and cook on HIGH 2½ to 3 hours. Remove mold from slow cooker. Let stand 10 minutes in mold. Transfer to cooling rack.

Fruits & Desserts

You can make many delicious desserts in your slow cooker. Actually, several types of desserts are perfectly suited because the slow cooker brings out those good old-fashioned flavors. It's hard to beat the taste of a fruit compote prepared in a slow cooker. Long cooking at very low temperatures blends the fruit flavors with the spices, wines or liqueurs.

Fresh or dried fruits may be used in many combinations, depending on what's available in your market. Dried fruits are especially good when prepared in a slow cooker. Firm fruits like apples and pears are also well suited to slow cooking. Baked Apples and St. Helena Pears bring out their fall flavors.

If you have never tried real homemade mincemeat, try Gar's Famous Mincemeat recipe. It is a variation of an old Pennsylvania Dutch mince pie. Don't be frightened by the long list of ingredients. Cut the recipe in half if you want to start off on a smaller scale.

Traditional Apple Butter is so easy to make in a slow cooker. In the past you had to stir it almost constantly to keep it from sticking and scorching. That was before electric slow cookers with low and even temperatures.

And, you can "bake" custard in a slow cooker. With Grandma's Rice Pudding or Trade Winds Baked Custard, turn the control to HIGH. The custardy mixture must be cooked on a trivet in hot water, so the trick is to cook it on HIGH.

I've included more steamed recipes in this section, such as Kahlua Bread Pudding. Before starting one of these, be sure you have a mold that will fit in your slow cooker. Or, you can cut some of the recipes down to fit your pot. To buy a mold to use in your slow cooker, measure the inside of your pot carefully, then take your tape measure with you when you shop.

Apple Peanut Crumble

Makes 5 or 6 servings

Topping with a slight peanut butter flavor provides an interesting contrast to the apples.

5 cooking apples, peeled, cored and sliced
⅔ cup packed brown sugar
½ cup all-purpose flour
½ cup quick-cooking rolled oats
½ teaspoon ground cinnamon
½ teaspoon freshly grated nutmeg
⅓ cup margarine or butter, room temperature
2 tablespoons peanut butter

Place apple slices in a slow cooker. In a medium bowl, combine sugar, flour, oats, cinnamon and nutmeg. Mix in margarine or butter and peanut butter with a pastry blender or fork until crumbly. Sprinkle over apples. Cover and cook on LOW 5 to 6 hours. Serve warm, plain or with ice cream or whipped cream.

Kahlua Bread Pudding

Makes 6 to 8 servings

If you have a 4- or 5-quart slow cooker, create this updated version of a traditional dessert.

½ (16-oz.) loaf unsliced French bread
2 (12-oz.) cans evaporated skimmed milk or 3 cups half-and-half
¼ cup Kahlua liqueur
3 eggs
⅓ cup sugar
1 tablespoon powdered instant coffee
¼ teaspoon ground cinnamon
Toasted slivered or sliced almonds

Place a metal rack or trivet in a slow cooker. Grease an 8- to 9-cup baking dish that fits into a 4- or 5-quart slow cooker. With a sharp knife, remove crust from bread; discard or make into bread crumbs for another use. Cut bread into 1-inch cubes; set aside. In a blender or food processor, combine milk or half-and-half, Kahlua, eggs, sugar, powdered coffee and cinnamon. Process until well mixed. Add to bread cubes. Stir to blend.

Fill prepared baking dish with mixture; cover with foil. Add 2 cups hot water to slow cooker. Place mold on rack in slow cooker. Cover and cook on HIGH 2 to 2½ hours or until a knife inserted in the pudding comes out clean. Serve warm or cool. Sprinkle with toasted almonds.

Nectarine Chutney

Makes about 5 cups

 Serve warm or cold, and create a spicy accent for broiled chicken or fish.

2 cups chopped fresh nectarines or peeled peaches
2 cups chopped peeled apples
1 small onion, chopped
½ cup dried cherries
½ cup golden raisins
1 tablespoon honey
½ cup cider vinegar
¾ cup packed brown sugar
¼ teaspoon ground cinnamon
¼ teaspoon red (cayenne) pepper
¼ teaspoon ground cloves
1 teaspoon ground ginger
1 teaspoon mustard seeds

Combine all ingredients in a slow cooker. Cover and cook on LOW 4 to 6 hours. Serve warm or cold. To keep chutney, place in a covered container and refrigerate. It will keep for weeks.

Fresh Mango Chutney
Makes 2 cups

Serve this savory condiment with your favorite chicken recipe, or as an accompaniment to curry.

½ cup cider vinegar
¾ cup packed brown sugar
1 tablespoon finely chopped gingerroot
½ teaspoon ground allspice
¼ teaspoon freshly grated nutmeg
½ teaspoon dried red pepper flakes
1 onion, finely chopped
½ teaspoon grated lemon peel
½ cup golden raisins
2 mangoes, peeled and coarsely chopped

Combine all ingredients in a slow cooker. Cover and cook on HIGH 2 hours, then simmer uncovered on HIGH an additional 2 hours or until mixture becomes syrupy. Cool to room temperature or refrigerate before serving. To keep chutney, place in a covered container and refrigerate. It will keep for weeks.

Down-Home Rhubarb
Makes about 3½ cups

During rhubarb season, double or triple this recipe and keep it in the refrigerator for snacking.

2 lbs. fresh rhubarb
1½ cups sugar
½ cup water
½ teaspoon vanilla extract (optional)

Trim rhubarb and cut into 1-inch pieces; place in a slow cooker. Dissolve sugar in water; pour over rhubarb. Cover and cook on LOW about 3 hours or until tender. Add vanilla if desired. Chill before serving.

Homestyle Applesauce
Makes 3½ to 4 cups

This applesauce will be slightly chunky. Put through a food processor or blender for a smoother texture.

8 to 9 medium cooking apples, peeled, cored and finely chopped
½ cup water
¾ cup sugar
Ground cinnamon

In a slow cooker, combine apples and water. Cover and cook on LOW about 6 hours or until apples are very soft. Add sugar and cook on LOW another 30 minutes. Sprinkle with cinnamon at serving time.

Chocolate Fondue

Makes 3 cups

When the slow cooker is turned on LOW, it keeps this chocolate mixture at just the right temperature for each person to dip his or her favorite treat.

6 (1-oz.) squares unsweetened chocolate
1½ cups sugar
1 cup half-and-half
½ cup margarine or butter
⅛ teaspoon salt
3 tablespoons crème de cacao or coffee-flavored liqueur
Angel cake cubes
Marshmallows
Fruits (strawberries, bananas, etc.)

Place chocolate in a slow cooker. Cover and heat on HIGH about 30 minutes or until chocolate melts. Stir in sugar, half-and-half, margarine or butter and salt. Cook on HIGH, stirring occasionally, 10 to 15 minutes. Whisk until smooth. Add liqueur. Turn control to LOW. Spear cake chunks, marshmallows or fruits with fondue forks. Dip into hot chocolate mixture.

Stewed Pears with Ginger

Makes 4 or 5 servings

 A simple dessert that's not too sweet. Bosc or Anjou pears work best.

1 cup vermouth
½ cup orange juice
2 tablespoons fresh lemon juice
½ cup plus 1 teaspoon sugar
1 tablespoon minced crystallized ginger
4 to 5 firm pears
1 (3-oz.) package cream cheese, room temperature
3 tablespoons chopped almonds or pecans
2 to 3 tablespoons vermouth or milk

In a slow cooker, combine vermouth, orange juice, lemon juice, ½ cup of the sugar, and ginger. Peel, halve and core pears. Drop into vermouth mixture and stir. Be sure pears are covered with liquid. Cover and cook on LOW 2 to 3 hours or until pears are tender. In a small bowl, mix cream cheese, nuts, milk, or vermouth and remaining 1 teaspoon sugar until well blended. Spoon pears and juice into bowls. Top with cream cheese mixture.

St. Helena Pears

Makes 6 servings

Macaroon crumbs add a little crunch to this rich, fruity dessert. For an exciting taste contrast, top each serving with a dollop of sour cream.

6 pears
½ cup raisins
¼ cup packed brown sugar
1 teaspoon grated lemon peel
¼ cup brandy
½ cup Sauterne wine
½ cup macaroon crumbs

Peel, halve and core pears; cut into thin slices. Mix raisins with sugar and lemon peel. Arrange alternately with pear slices in a slow cooker. Pour brandy and wine over pears. Cover and cook on LOW 4 to 6 hours or until pears are tender. Spoon pears into serving dishes and allow to cool. Sprinkle with crumbs.

Chocolate Mint Dessert
Makes 4 to 6 servings

Instead of whipped cream, top with vanilla ice cream and a fresh raspberry sauce.

1 cup sugar
¼ cup margarine or butter, room temperature
1 egg
3 tablespoons all-purpose flour
1 cup fine dry bread crumbs
1½ teaspoons baking powder
¾ cup evaporated milk
2 oz. unsweetened chocolate, melted
1 teaspoon peppermint extract
¼ cup chopped walnuts
Whipped cream (optional)

Place a metal rack or trivet in a slow cooker. Grease a 1-quart mold or metal bowl. In a large bowl, cream sugar, margarine or butter, and egg. Combine flour, bread crumbs and baking powder. Mix in flour mixture alternately with milk. Stir in melted chocolate, peppermint extract and walnuts. Pour into prepared mold. Cover with foil; crimp edges to seal. Add 2 cups water to slow cooker. Place mold on rack in slow cooker. Cover and cook on HIGH 2 to 3 hours. Serve warm or cold, topped with whipped cream, if desired.

Rosy Cinnamon Applesauce

Makes 2 cups

 The candies provide color, flavor and sweetening—all so amazingly simple.

¼ cup hot water
½ cup red hot candies
4 to 5 large Granny Smith apples
¼ cup sugar

In a slow cooker, combine hot water and red hot candies. Let stand 10 minutes. Peel, core and finely chop apples. Stir apples and sugar into water and red hots until thoroughly combined. Cover and cook on HIGH 3 to 4 hours. If a smooth sauce is desired, process in a blender or food processor until pureed. Serve warm or cold.

Homestyle Bread Pudding

Makes 6 servings

Here's a basic pudding that you can vary by using other dried fruit or even substituting chocolate chips.

1 (14-oz.) can sweetened condensed milk
1¾ cups water
2 eggs, slightly beaten
1 teaspoon vanilla extract
½ teaspoon ground cinnamon
3½ cups 1-inch bread cubes
½ cup chopped dates or raisins

RUM SAUCE
2 tablespoons sugar
2 tablespoons cornstarch
1 cup apple juice
½ cup rum

Place a metal rack or trivet in a slow cooker. Grease a 1-quart baking dish or metal bowl. In a large bowl, beat together milk, water, eggs, vanilla and cinnamon. Add bread cubes and dates or raisins. Thoroughly mix; let stand 10 minutes. Spoon into prepared baking dish. Add ½ cup water to slow cooker. Set baking dish on rack. Cover and cook on HIGH 2½ to 3 hours. Remove from slow cooker and let stand 15 minutes before serving. Prepare Rum Sauce and serve with pudding.

Rum Sauce

Makes about 1¹/₂ cups

In a saucepan, mix together sugar, cornstarch and apple juice. Cook over low heat, stirring, until slightly thickened. Remove from heat; stir in rum. Serve warm or cold.

Fruit Medley

Makes 5 or 6 servings

For a different final touch, whip sour cream with sugar to taste and a sprinkle of nutmeg.

1½ lbs. mixed dried fruits
2½ cups water
1 cup sugar
1 tablespoon honey
Peel of ½ lemon, cut into thin strips
⅛ teaspoon freshly grated nutmeg
1 cinnamon stick
3 tablespoons cornstarch
¼ cup Cointreau

Put dried fruit into a slow cooker. Pour in water. Stir in sugar, honey, lemon peel and spices. Cover and cook on LOW 2 to 3 hours. Turn control to HIGH. In small amount of water, mix cornstarch; stir into fruit mixture. Cover and cook on HIGH 10 minutes or until thickened. Add Cointreau. Serve warm or chilled. May be served as fruit compote or as topping for ice cream.

Gar's Famous Mincemeat

Makes 3 qts. mincemeat or enough for four 9-inch pies

My husband, Gar, worked diligently to produce this family favorite. All early mincemeat recipes contained meat, as this one does.

2½ lbs. beef shanks
4 cups water
½ lb. beef suet
2 lbs. tart apples, peeled and diced
1 (15-oz.) package raisins
1 (11-oz.) package currants
1 tablespoon grated lemon peel
1 tablespoon fresh lemon juice
1 tablespoon grated orange peel
¼ cup orange juice
1 teaspoon cinnamon
½ teaspoon ground cloves
½ teaspoon freshly grated nutmeg
1 teaspoon salt
2 cups molasses
½ cup packed brown sugar
1½ cups apple cider

Combine beef and water in a slow cooker. Cover and cook on LOW 8 to 10 hours. Save all the broth; remove beef from bones. In food chopper, grind beef and suet together. Combine beef with ½ cup of reserved broth and remaining ingredients in slow cooker. Cover and cook on LOW 8 to 10 hours.

When making pies, 2 or 3 tablespoons brandy or bourbon may be added to filling for each pie. Filling can be kept in refrigerator for several days or frozen for about 6 months. Extra broth can be used for a soup base.

Apple Brown Betty

Makes 4 or 5 servings

 For a special treat, top this dessert with light cream or a scoop of ice cream.

5 slices bread, cut into ½-inch cubes
½ cup margarine or butter, melted
½ teaspoon ground cinnamon
¼ teaspoon freshly grated nutmeg
⅛ teaspoon salt
¾ cup packed brown sugar
4 medium cooking apples, peeled, cored and chopped

In a medium bowl, mix bread cubes with margarine or butter, cinnamon, nutmeg, salt and brown sugar. Arrange in alternate layers with apples in a slow cooker. Cover and cook on HIGH 1½ to 2½ hours or until apples are tender. Serve warm.

Apple-Cranberry Compote
Makes 5 or 6 servings

Fresh crisp apples and tart cranberries in the market mean that fall has arrived and it's time for making fruit compotes.

5 to 6 cooking apples, peeled, cored and sliced
1 cup fresh cranberries
1 cup sugar
½ teaspoon grated orange peel
½ cup cranberry-raspberry juice
¼ cup Port wine
Sour cream

Put apple slices and cranberries into a slow cooker. Sprinkle sugar over fruit. Add orange peel, juice and wine. Stir to mix ingredients. Cover and cook on LOW 4 to 6 hours or until apples are tender. Serve warm fruits with the juices, topped with a dab of sour cream.

Holiday Fruit Compote

Makes 4 to 6 servings

If you wish this dessert to be nonalcoholic, substitute apple or cranberry juice for the wine.

¼ cup Port wine
1 tablespoon margarine or butter
1¼ cups sugar
1 tablespoon grated lemon peel
⅛ teaspoon ground cinnamon
⅛ teaspoon freshly grated nutmeg
4 medium apples, peeled, cored and sliced
2 cups fresh cranberries
½ cup chopped pitted dates
⅓ cup chopped walnuts
Sour cream or ice cream

In a slow cooker, combine wine, margarine or butter, sugar, lemon peel and spices. Add apples and cranberries. Cover and cook on LOW 4 to 6 hours. Stir in dates and walnuts. Serve warm or cold with a dollop of sour cream or use as a sauce for ice cream.

Orange-Prune Compote

Makes 8 to 10 servings

Serve this at your next brunch. Your guests will appreciate a change from the usual fare.

1 lb. pitted dried prunes
3 cups water
2 (11-oz.) cans mandarin oranges, drained
⅓ cup sugar
¼ cup Cointreau or Curaçao
½ cup orange juice
2 bananas, sliced

Combine prunes with water in a slow cooker. Cover and cook on LOW 2 to 2½ hours. Cool and drain. Combine with mandarin oranges, sugar, Cointreau and orange juice. Cover and refrigerate several hours before serving. Just before serving, stir in bananas.

Baked Apples

Makes 5 or 6 servings

 Use fresh, crisp apples for this wintertime treat.

5 to 6 baking apples, such as Rome Beauty or Granny Smith
½ cup raisins or chopped dates
1 cup packed brown sugar
1 cup boiling water
2 tablespoons margarine or butter
½ teaspoon ground cinnamon
¼ teaspoon freshly grated nutmeg

Core apples and peel each about one quarter of the way down. Arrange in a slow cooker. Fill centers with raisins or dates. In a small bowl, combine sugar, water, margarine or butter, cinnamon and nutmeg. Pour over apples. Cover and cook on LOW 2 to 4 hours (depending on size and variety of apples) or until apples are tender. Serve warm or cool.

Grandma's Rice Pudding

Makes 6 to 8 servings

 When I was a child, my mother would sometimes make this for my lunch.

⅔ cup uncooked long-grain rice
1⅓ cups water
2 cups milk
2 tablespoons margarine or butter
¼ teaspoon salt
⅓ cup sugar
2 eggs, beaten
1 teaspoon vanilla extract
¾ cup raisins
Ground cinnamon

Place a metal rack or trivet in a slow cooker. Grease a 5- or 6-cup baking dish. Cook rice according to package directions using 1⅓ cups water. Combine cooked rice with milk, margarine or butter, salt, sugar, eggs, vanilla and raisins. Pour into prepared baking dish. Cover baking dish with foil. Add 1 cup hot water to slow cooker. Place baking dish on trivet. Cover and cook on HIGH 4 hours. Sprinkle with cinnamon. Serve warm. Refrigerate any leftovers and serve chilled.

Traditional Apple Butter
Makes about 8 cups

When apples are in season, buy, or better yet, pick a large amount of fruit and make your own butter.

12 to 14 cooking apples (about 16 cups chopped)
2 cups apple cider
2 cups sugar
1 teaspoon ground cinnamon
¼ teaspoon ground cloves

Core and chop apples. (Do not peel.) Combine apples and cider in a slow cooker. Cover and cook on LOW 10 to 12 hours or until apples are mushy. Puree in a food mill or sieve. Return pureed mixture to slow cooker. Add sugar, cinnamon and cloves. Cover and cook on LOW 1 hour.

NOTE: Apple butter will keep several weeks in the refrigerator. For longer storage, can in sterilized jars following proper canning procedures or pour into freezer containers and freeze.

Trade Winds Baked Custard

Makes 5 or 6 servings

Traditional baked custard becomes exotic when it is adorned with a tropical topping.

3 eggs, beaten slightly
⅓ cup sugar
1 teaspoon vanilla extract
2 cups milk
⅛ teaspoon freshly grated nutmeg
Trade Winds Topping (see below)
Toasted coconut

TRADE WINDS TOPPING
1 large mango, peeled and chopped
½ teaspoon minced crystallized ginger
¼ teaspoon Chinese five spice powder

Place a metal rack or trivet in a slow cooker. Grease a 1-quart baking dish. In a medium bowl, combine eggs, sugar and vanilla. Stir in milk. Pour into prepared dish. Sprinkle with nutmeg. Cover dish with foil. Add 2 cups hot water to slow cooker. Place filled dish on rack. Cover and cook on HIGH 2½ to 3 hours or until firm. Refrigerate until cool. Prepare topping and spoon over custard; sprinkle with coconut.

Trade Winds Topping

Combine mango, ginger and Chinese five spice powder in a bowl.

Index

A

Acorn Squash, Indonesian, 188
Algerian Lamb Shanks, 113
All-American Snack, 13
Almonds
   Algerian Lamb Shanks, 113
   Curried Almonds, 15
   Kahlua Bread Pudding, 220
    Mission Chicken, 134
   Stewed Pears with Ginger, 225
Appetizers & Beverages, 7–24
Apple Brown Betty, 232
Apple butter
   Traditional Apple Butter, 238
Apple Cider
   Gar's Famous Mincement, 231
   Mulled Cider, 20
   Padre Punch, 17
   Traditional Apple Butter, 238
Apple jelly
   Rathskeller Pork, 101
Apple juice
   Rum Sauce, 229
   Shades of Autumn Rice, 196
Apple Peanut Crumble, 219
Apple-Cranberry Compote, 233
Apples
   Apple Brown Betty, 232
   Apple Peanut Crumble, 219

Apple-Cranberry Compote, 233
Baked Apples, 236
Buck County's Spareribs, 97
Gar's Famous Mincemeat, 231
Holiday Fruit Compote, 234
Homestyle Applesauce, 223
Kielbasa & Napa Cabbage, 110
Nectarine Chutney, 221
Orange Barley Casserole, 194
Rathskeller Pork, 101
Rosy Cinnamon Applesauce, 228
Shades of Autumn Rice, 196
Traditional Apple Butter, 238
Apricot nectar
   Spiced Apricot Punch, 16
Apricots
   Algerian Lamb Shanks, 113
   Fruited Lamb Roll, 111
   Orange Barley Casserole, 194
   Persimmon Pudding, 202
Arroz con Pollo, 127
Artichoke hearts
   Eggplant-Artichoke Parmigiana, 179
   Fiesta Turkey & Bean Salad, 161
Autumn Pork Chops, 102
Avocado

Slow-Cooker Fajitas, 64

B

Bacon
   Beef Burgundy, 77
   Corn-Bacon Pudding, 176
   Flemish Carbonades, 60
   Fresh Black-eyed Peas, 164
   Knockwurst with Hot German Potato Salad, 109
   Lentil Casserole, 194
   Mac's Kidney Beans, 169
   Rhineland Sweet-Sour Cabbage, 173
   Sweet-Sour Bean Trio, 166
   Welsh Rarebit, 54
Baja Beef 'n' Beans, 82
Baked Apples, 236
Baking, 6
Bamboo shoots
   Cashew Chicken, 119
Banana chips
   Tropical Bread with Brandy Hard Sauce, 212
Bananas
   Banana Nut Bread, 207
   Orange-Prune Compote, 235
Barbecue Beef Sandwiches, 50
Barbecued Spareribs, 99
Barley
   Curried Barley, 193
   Orange Barley Casserole, 194

Bean sprouts
Chicken Chop Suey, 132
Chinese Pepper Steak, 83
Gingery Beef Strips, 87
Beans, 155–170
Beans
Baja Beef 'n' Beans, 82
Beef Burritos, 58
Black Bean Chili with Pork, 107
Chili con Carne, 79
Confetti Bean Casserole, 162
Congressional Bean Soup, 45
Favorite Baked Beans, 163
Fennel-Bean Soup, 27
Fiesta Turkey & Bean Salad, 161
Hot Sausage & Bean Stew, 160
Mac's Kidney Beans, 169
Minestrone Soup, 32
Pizza Beans, 165
Red Beans & Rice, 157
Refried Bean Dip, 12
Refried Black Beans, 158
Savory Tomato Limas, 168
Short-Cut Turkey Chili, 152
Sloppy Jane Sandwiches, 51
Slow-Cooker Cassoulet, 170
Sour Cream Limas, 167
Southwest Beef & Pintos, 159
Sweet-Sour Bean Trio, 166
Vegetarian Sauce, 198
Beef, 55–92
Beef
Baja Beef 'n' Beans, 82
Barbecue Beef Sandwiches, 50
Beef Burgundy, 77
Beef Burritos, 58
Beef Stroganoff, 91
Black Forest Pot Roast, 57
California Tamale Pie, 67
Cheddar Cheese Meat Loaf, 68
Chili con Carne, 79
Chinese Pepper Steak, 83
Corned Beef, 65
Creole-Asian Strips, 85
Family Favorite Meat Loaf, 69
Farm-style Stew, 80
Favorite Pot Roast, 59
Flank Steak in Mushroom

Wine Sauce, 86
Flemish Carbonades, 60
Gar's Famous Mincemeat, 231
German Short Ribs, 74
Gingery Beef Strips, 87
Glazed Corned Beef, 65
Hamburger Soup, 31
Hearty Alphabet Soup, 37
Home-style Short Ribs, 75
Hungarian Goulash, 81
Italian Meatball Stew, 70
Lentil Soup, Crescenti Style, 28
Marco Polo Short Ribs, 76
Minestrone Soup, 32
New England Chuck Roast, 90
Old World Sauerbraten, 61
Old-Fashioned Beef Stew, 89
Oxtail Soup, 33
Pot Roast with Creamy Mushroom Sauce, 62
Scandinavian Dilled Pot Roast, 63
Shell Casserole, 71
Sloppy Joes, 52
Slow-Cooker Fajitas, 64
Southwest Beef & Pintos, 159
Spaghetti Meat Sauce, 72
Spicy Brisket over Noodles, 66
Stuffed Flank Steak with Currant Wine Sauce, 88
Stuffed Green Peppers, 184
Swedish Cabbage Rolls, 73
Swiss-style Beef Birds, 84
Teriyaki Steak, 78
Flemish Carbonades, 60
Spicy Brisket over Noodles, 66
Beer
Tavern Soup, 42
Welsh Rarebit, 54
Before you start cooking, 6
Bell peppers
Black Bean Chili with Pork, 107
Chinese Pepper Steak, 83
Confetti Bean Casserole, 162
Creole Zucchini, 192
Fiesta Turkey & Bean Salad, 161
Red & Gold Sweet-Sour

Chicken, 139
Red Beans & Rice, 157
Slow-Cooker Fajitas, 64
Stuffed Green Peppers, 184
Biscuit mix
Nostalgic Chicken & Herbed Dumplings, 137
Bishop's Wine, 23
Black Bean Chili with Pork, 107
Black Forest Pot Roast, 57
Black-eyed peas
Fresh Black-eyed Peas, 164
Blueberries
Blueberry & Orange Bread, 208
Blueberry Brown Bread, 213
Blueberry Coffee Cake, 205
Bouillabaisse, 49
Brandy
St. Helena Pears, 226
Bread crumbs
Chocolate Mint Dessert, 227
Chocolate Pudding Cake, 204
Ground Turkey Vegetable Round, 153
Bread stuffing
Corn-Stuffed Pork Chops, 103
Stuffed Flank Steak with Currant Wine Sauce, 88
Breads & Cakes, 199–215
Breads
Banana Nut Bread, 207
Blueberry & Orange Bread, 208
Blueberry Brown Bread, 213
Cornbread, 209
Date & Nut Loaf, 215
Peanut Butter Bread, 211
Pumpkin Nut Bread, 214
Steamed Molasses Bread, 210
Tropical Bread with Brandy Hard Sauce, 212
Buck County's Spareribs, 97
Burgundy-basted Duckling, 143
Buttermilk
Blueberry Brown Bread, 213
Pumpkin Nut Bread, 214
Steamed Molasses Bread, 210

C

Cabbage
Kielbasa & Napa Cabbage, 110

Cabbage (*continued*)
Lentil Soup, Crescenti Style, 28
New England Chuck Roast, 90
Rathskeller Pork, 101
Rhineland Sweet-Sour Cabbage, 173
Swedish Cabbage Rolls, 73
Swedish Cabbage Soup, 39
Cacciatore
Chicken Cacciatore, 122
Cakes
Blueberry Coffee Cake, 205
Carrot Coffee Cake, 206
Chocolate Pudding Cake, 204
Calabacitas, 191
California Tamale Pie, 67
Candied fruits
Traditional Plum Pudding, 201
Caraway seeds
Kielbasa & Napa Cabbage, 110
Rathskeller Pork, 101
Swiss-style Beef Birds, 84
Caribbean "Jerked" Chicken, 120
Carrots
Carrot Coffee Cake, 206
Carrots in Dilled Wine Sauce, 174
Favorite Pot Roast, 59
Homestyle Short Ribs, 75
Lemon Parsnips & Carrots, 183
New England Chuck Roast, 90
Old-Fashioned Beef Stew, 89
Orange-Glazed Ginger Carrots, 175
Cashews
Cashew Chicken, 119
East Indian Snack, 14
Celery seeds
Barbecued Spareribs, 99
Cereals
All-American Snack, 13
East Indian Snack, 14
Steamed Molasses Bread, 210
Cheddar Cheese Meat Loaf, 68
Cheese
California Tamale Pie, 67
Cheddar Cheese Meat Loaf, 68
Chicken Breasts, Saltimbocca Style, 124

Chicken Olé, 128
Chicken Tetrazzini, 126
Chicken Tortilla Casserole, 130
Corn-Bacon Pudding, 176
Couscous Provençal, 195
Ham-Stuffed French Rolls, 53
Leeks au Gratin, 181
Mock Chile Relleno, 178
Pizza Beans, 165
Potato Soup, Florentine Style, 29
Refried Bean Dip, 12
Refried Black Beans, 158
Short-Cut Chili con Queso, 12
Tavern Soup, 42
Touch of Green Soup with Goat Cheese Topping, 30
Turkey Lasagna, 151
Welsh Rarebit, 54
Cherries
Cornish Hens with Cherry Sauce, 141
Nectarine Chutney, 221
Chicken
Arroz con Pollo, 127
Caribbean "Jerked" Chicken, 120
Cashew Chicken, 119
Chicken & Leek Terrine, 10
Chicken Breasts, Saltimbocca Style, 124
Chicken Cacciatore, 122
Chicken Chop Suey, 132
Chicken Olé, 128
Chicken Tetrazzini, 126
Chicken Tortilla Casserole, 130
Chinese Roast Chicken, 129
Curried Island Chicken, 133
Jambalaya, 140
Kowloon Chicken, 121
Mission Chicken, 134
North-of-the-Border Pozole, 129
Nostalgic Chicken & Herbed Dumplings, 137
Paella, 135
Red & Gold Sweet-Sour Chicken, 139
Slow-Cooker Cassoulet, 170
Sorrento Chicken Roll-ups, 125

Tarragon Chicken Thighs, 138
Thai Chicken, 136
Tortilla Soup, 43
Touch-of-the-Orient Chicken Rolls, 131
Venetian Chicken, 123
Chiles
Beef Burritos, 58
Calabacitas, 191
Caribbean "Jerked" Chicken, 120
Chicken Tortilla Casserole, 130
Chili con Carne, 79
Hot Sausage & Bean Stew, 160
Jalapeño Pesto, 36
Mock Chile Relleno, 178
North-of-the-Border Pozole, 129
Red Beans & Rice, 157
Short-Cut Chili con Queso, 12
Slow-Cooker Fajitas, 64
Southwest Beef & Pintos, 159
Sweet-Hot Pumpkin Soup, 35
Tortilla Soup, 43
Chili con Carne, 79
Chili Dogs, 51
Chili Nuts, 15
Chili sauce
Mac's Kidney Beans, 169
Sloppy Jane Sandwiches, 51
Sloppy Joes, 52
Chili seasoning
Chili Nuts, 15
Chili
Black Bean Chili with Pork, 107
Short-Cut Turkey Chili, 152
Chinese Pepper Steak, 83
Chinese Roast Chicken, 129
Chinese-style Country Ribs, 97
Chocolate
Chocolate Fondue, 224
Chocolate Mint Dessert, 227
Chocolate Pudding Cake, 204
Mediterranean Coffee, 22
Chops
Autumn Pork Chops, 102
Corn-Stuffed Pork Chops, 103
Hawaiian Pork Chops, 104
Plantation Pork Chops, 105

Chutney
Acorn Squash, Indonesian, 188
Fresh Mango Chutney, 222
Nectarine Chutney, 221
Cinnamon bread
Cornish Hens with Lime Glaze, 142
Cinnamon sticks
Bishop's Wine, 23
Cranberry Wine Punch, 16
Fruit Medley, 230
Hot Buttered Rum Punch, 18
Mediterranean Coffee, 22
Padre Punch, 17
Spiced Apricot Punch, 16
Tropical Tea, 19
Clam juice
New England Clam Chowder, 48
Clams
New England Clam Chowder, 48
Paella, 135
Cleaning your slow cooker, 6
Cloves
Bishop's Wine, 23
Cranberry Wine Punch, 16
Crockery Ham, 108
Mediterranean Coffee, 22
Mulled Cider, 20
Padre Punch, 17
Coconut
Acorn Squash, Indonesian, 188
East Indian Snack, 14
Hawaiian Pork Chops, 104
Trade Winds Baked Custard, 239
Coffee
Mediterranean Coffee, 22
Cognac
Marinated Leg of Lamb, 112
Compotes
Apple-Cranberry Compote, 233
Holiday Fruit Compote, 234
Orange-Prune Compote, 235
Confetti Bean Casserole, 162
Congressional Bean Soup, 45
Cooking times, 4
Corn Stuffing Balls, 177
Corn-Bacon Pudding, 176
Corn-Stuffed Pork Chops, 103
Cornbread stuffing

Cornish Hens with Cherry Sauce, 141
Plantation Pork Chops, 105
Stuffed Flank Steak, 88
Cornbread, 209
Corn
Calabacitas, 191
California Tamale Pie, 67
Confetti Bean Casserole, 162
Corn Stuffing Balls, 177
Corn-Bacon Pudding, 176
Corn-Stuffed Pork Chops, 103
Down East Corn Chowder, 47
Farm-style Stew, 80
Stuffed Green Peppers, 184
Corned Beef, 65
Cornish Hens with Cherry Sauce, 141
Cornish Hens with Lime Glaze, 142
Cornmeal
Blueberry Brown Bread, 213
California Tamale Pie, 67
Cornbread, 209
Sausage Polenta Pie, 154
Couscous
Algerian Lamb Shanks, 113
Couscous Provençal, 195
Cran-Orange Turkey Roll, 147
Cranberries
Apple-Cranberry Compote, 233
Cran-Orange Turkey Roll, 147
Cranberry Pork Roast, 106
Fruited Lamb Roll, 111
Holiday Fruit Compote, 234
Orange-Cranberry Turkey Fettucine, 145
Cranberry juice
Cranberry Wine Punch, 16
Cranberry sauce
Hot Buttered Rum Punch, 18
Cranberry Wine Punch, 16
Cream cheese
Stewed Pears with Ginger, 225
Cream of chicken soup
Chicken Breasts, Saltimbocca Style, 124
Chicken Olé, 128
Cream of mushroom soup
Chicken Olé, 128

Pot Roast with Creamy Mushroom Sauce, 62
Creole Zucchini, 192
Creole-Asian Strips, 85
Crockery Ham, 108
Crumble
Apple Peanut Crumble, 219
Currant jelly
Cornish Hens with Cherry Sauce, 141
Crockery Ham, 108
Imperial Duckling, 144
Stuffed Flank Steak with Currant Wine Sauce, 88
Currants
Gar's Famous Mincemeat, 231
Orange Barley Casserole, 194
Curry powder
Curried Almonds, 15
Curried Barley, 193
Curried Island Chicken, 133
East Indian Snack, 14
Sweet-Hot Pumpkin Soup, 35
Custard
Trade Winds Baked Custard, 239

D

Dates
Date & Nut Loaf, 215
Holiday Fruit Compote, 234
Homestyle Bread Pudding, 229
Orange Barley Casserole, 194
Dill pickles
Swiss-style Beef Birds, 84
Dill
Carrots in Dilled Wine Sauce, 174
Fiesta Turkey & Bean Salad, 161
Hungarian Goulash, 81
Scandinavian Dilled Pot Roast, 63
Down East Corn Chowder, 47
Down-Home Rhubarb, 223
Dried fruits
Fruit Medley, 230
Duck
Burgundy-basted Duckling, 143
Imperial Duckling, 144

Dumplings
  Nostalgic Chicken & Herbed
    Dumplings, 137

E

East Indian Snack, 14
Eggplant
  Eggplant-Artichoke
    Parmigiana, 179
  Mediterranean Caponata, 9
  Party-style Ratatouille, 11

F

Fajitas
  Slow-Cooker Fajitas, 64
Family Favorite Meat Loaf, 69
Farm-style Stew, 80
Favorite Baked Beans, 163
Favorite Pot Roast, 59
Fennel-Bean Soup, 27
Fiesta Turkey & Bean Salad, 161
Fish
  Bouillabaisse, 49
Five spice powder
  Chinese Roast Chicken, 129
  Creole-Asian Strips, 85
  Lentil Casserole, 194
  Trade Winds Baked Custard,
    239
Flank Steak in Mushroom Wine
  Sauce, 86
Flemish Carbonades, 60
Fondue
  Chocolate Fondue, 224
French Onion Soup, 40
Fresh Black-eyed Peas, 164
Fresh Mango Chutney, 222
Frozen foods, 5
Fruit Medley, 230
Fruited Lamb Roll, 111
Fruits & Desserts, 217–239

G

Gar's Famous mincemeat, 231
Georgia Peanut Soup, 34
German Short Ribs, 74
Ginger
  Indonesian Pork, 95
  Stewed Pears with Ginger,
    225
  Trade Winds Baked Custard,
    239
Gingerroot
  Caribbean "Jerked" Chicken,
    120

Cashew Chicken, 119
Chicken Chop Suey, 132
Chinese Roast Chicken, 129
Fruited Lamb Roll, 111
Gingery Beef Strips, 87
Kowloon Chicken, 121
Orange-Glazed Ginger
  Carrots, 175
Southeast Asian-style
  Meatballs, 150
Teriyaki Steak, 78
Touch-of-the-Orient Chicken
  Rolls, 131
Fresh Mango Chutney, 222
Gingersnaps
  Old World Sauerbraten, 61
Gingery Beef Strips, 87
Glazed Corned Beef, 65
Golden Squash Soup with
  Pesto Topping, 36
Goulash
  Hungarian Goulash, 81
Grandma's Rice Pudding, 237
Grapes
  Mission Chicken, 134
Greek Herbed Lamb with Rice,
  114
Green Beans, Portuguese Style,
  180
Ground Turkey Vegetable
  Round, 153

H

Hamburger Soup, 31
Ham
  Chicken Breasts, Saltimbocca
    Style, 124
  Congressional Bean Soup, 45
  Crockery Ham, 108
  Ham-Stuffed French Rolls,
    53
  Homestead Ham Loaf, 96
  Potato Soup, Florentine
    Style, 29
  Split-Pea Soup, 38
Hawaiian Pork Chops, 104
Hearty Alphabet Soup, 37
Herbed Spinach Soup, 41
Herbed Squash Trio, 185
High-altitude cooking, 4
Hoisin sauce
  Red & Gold Sweet-Sour
    Chicken, 139
  Southeast Asian-style
    Meatballs, 150

Holiday Fruit Compote, 234
Homestead Ham Loaf, 96
Homestyle Applesauce, 223
Homestyle Bread Pudding,
  229
Homestyle Short Ribs, 75
Hominy
  North-of-the-Border Pozole,
    129
Honey
  Cranberry Pork Roast, 106
  Indonesian Pork, 95
  Soy-Glazed Spareribs, 98
  Stuffed Honeyed Sweet
    Potatoes, 186
Horseradish
  Glazed Corned Beef, 65
  Homestead Ham Loaf, 96
  Marco Polo Short Ribs, 76
  New England Chuck Roast,
    90
Hot Buttered Rum Punch, 18
Hot dogs
  Chili Dogs, 51
  Sloppy Jane Sandwiches, 51
Hot Lime Sauce, 202
Hot Mint Malt, 20
Hot Sausage & Bean Stew, 160
Hot Spiced Burgundy, 24
Hungarian Goulash, 81

I

Imperial Duckling, 144
Indonesian Pork, 95
Irish Lamb Stew, 116
Italian Meatball Stew, 70
Italian-style vegetables
  Hearty Alphabet Soup, 37
  Italian Meatball Stew, 70

J

Jalapeño Pesto, 36
Jambalaya, 140
Jicama
  Red & Gold Sweet-Sour
    Chicken, 139

K

Kahlua Bread Pudding, 220
Keep it covered, 4
Kielbasa & Napa Cabbage, 110
Killarney Chowder, 46
Knockwurst with Hot German
  Potato Salad, 109
Kowloon Chicken, 121

L

Lamb
Algerian Lamb Shanks, 113
Fruited Lamb Roll, 111
Greek Herbed Lamb with
Rice, 114
Irish Lamb Stew, 116
Marinated Leg of Lamb, 112
Mexican Lamb with Red
Wine, 115
Swedish Cabbage Soup, 39
Lasagna
Turkey Lasagna, 151
Leave it alone, 3
Leeks
Chicken & Leek Terrine, 10
Leeks au Gratin, 181
Oxtail Soup, 33
Swedish Cabbage Soup, 39
Touch of Green Soup with
Goat Cheese Topping, 30
Turkey with Leek & White
Wine Sauce, 148
Lemon Parsnips & Carrots,
183
Lemons
Cranberry Wine Punch, 16
Lentils
Lentil Casserole, 194
Lentil Soup, Crescenti Style,
28
Lettuce
Herbed Spinach Soup, 41
Lime juice
Cornish Hens with Lime
Glaze, 142
Hot Lime Sauce, 202
Lobster
Bouillabaisse, 49

M

Mac's Kidney Beans, 169
Macaroni
Hamburger Soup, 31
Minestrone Soup, 32
Malted milk powder
Hot Mint Malt, 20
Mangoes
Fresh Mango Chutney, 222
Kowloon Chicken, 121
Red & Gold Sweet-Sour
Chicken, 139
Trade Winds Baked Custard,
239

Tropical Bread with Brandy
Hard Sauce, 212
Maple syrup
Persimmon Pudding, 202
Marco Polo Short Ribs, 76
Marinara Sauce, 197
Marinated Leg of Lamb, 112
Marmalade
Chinese-style Country Ribs,
97
Cran-Orange Turkey Roll,
147
Orange-Glazed Ginger
Carrots, 175
Meat loaf
Cheddar Cheese Meat Loaf,
68
Family Favorite Meat Loaf,
69
Meat rack, 5
Meatballs
Italian Meatball Stew, 70
Southeast Asian-style
Meatballs, 150
Mediterranean Caponata, 9
Mediterranean Coffee, 22
Mexican Lamb with Red Wine,
115
Mincemeat
Gar's Famous Mincemeat,
231
Minestrone Soup, 32
Mint
Chocolate Mint Dessert, 227
Fruited Lamb Roll, 111
Greek Herbed Lamb with
Rice, 114
Lemon Parsnips & Carrots,
183
Mission Chicken, 134
Mock Chile Relleno, 178
Molasses
Blueberry Brown Bread, 213
Favorite Baked Beans, 163
Gar's Famous Mincemeat,
231
Glazed Corned Beef, 65
Sour Cream Limas, 167
Steamed Molasses Bread, 210
Turkey Fillets, Barbecue
Style, 149
Mulled Cider, 20
Mushrooms
Beef Burgundy, 77
Beef Stroganoff, 91

Black Forest Pot Roast, 57
Cashew Chicken, 119
Chicken Cacciatore, 122
Chicken Chop Suey, 132
Chicken Tetrazzini, 126
Flank Steak in Mushroom
Wine Sauce, 86
Shell Casserole, 71
Sorrento Chicken Roll-ups,
125
Stuffed Flank Steak with
Currant Wine Sauce, 88
Vegetarian Sauce, 198
Venetian Chicken, 123

N

Nectarine Chutney, 221
New England Chuck Roast, 90
New England Clam Chowder,
48
Noodles
Beef Burgundy, 77
East Indian Snack, 14
German Short Ribs, 74
Hearty Alphabet Soup, 37
Hungarian Goulash, 81
Orange-Cranberry Turkey
Fettucine, 145
Spicy Brisket over Noodles,
66
Turkey Lasagna, 151
Turkey Noodle Soup, 44
North-of-the-Border Pozole,
129
Nostalgic Chicken & Herbed
Dumplings, 137

O

Oats
Apple Peanut Crumble, 219
Homestead Ham Loaf, 96
Old World Sauerbraten, 61
Old-Fashioned Beef Stew, 89
Old-Fashioned Stewed
Tomatoes, 190
Olives
Arroz con Pollo, 127
California Tamale Pie, 67
Couscous Provençal, 195
Ham-Stuffed French Rolls,
53
Mediterranean Caponata, 9
Onion soup mix
Hamburger Soup, 31
Hearty Alphabet Soup, 37

Onion soup mix (*continued*)
   Pot Roast with Creamy
      Mushroom Sauce, 62
Onions
   French Onion Soup, 40
   Nostalgic Chicken & Herbed
      Dumplings, 137
   Old-Fashioned Beef Stew, 89
   Sweet-Sour Baby Onions,
      182
Orange Barley Casserole, 194
Orange juice
   Algerian Lamb Shanks, 113
   Blueberry & Orange Bread,
      208
   Imperial Duckling, 144
   Mission Chicken, 134
   Orange Barley Casserole, 194
   Orange-Cranberry Turkey
      Fettucine, 145
   Orange-Prune Compote, 235
   Padre Punch, 17
   Plantation Pork Chops, 105
   Stewed Pears with Ginger,
      225
   Tropical Bread with Brandy
      Hard Sauce, 212
   Tropical Tea, 19
Orange-Cranberry Turkey
   Fettucine, 145
Orange-Glazed Ginger Carrots,
   175
Orange-Prune Compote, 235
Orange
   Bishop's Wine, 23
   Imperial Duckling, 144
   Mulled Cider, 20
   Orange-Prune Compote, 235
   Touch-of-the-Orient Chicken
      Rolls, 131
   Tropical Tea, 19
Oxtail Soup, 33

P

Padre Punch, 17
Paella, 135
Papaya
   Hawaiian Pork Chops, 104
Paprika
   Hungarian Goulash, 81
Parsnips
   Lemon Parsnips & Carrots,
      183
   Swedish Cabbage Soup, 39
Party-style Ratatouille, 11

Pasta
   Chicken Cacciatore, 122
   Shell Casserole, 71
   Sorrento Chicken Roll-ups,
      125
   Venetian Chicken, 123
Pea pods
   Cashew Chicken, 119
   Gingery Beef Strips, 87
Peanut butter
   Apple Peanut Crumble, 219
   Georgia Peanut Soup, 34
   Indonesian Pork, 95
   Peanut Butter Bread, 211
Peanuts
   All-American Snack, 13
   Chili Nuts, 15
Pears
   St. Helena Pears, 226
   Stewed Pears with Ginger,
      225
Peas
   Arroz con Pollo, 127
   Irish Lamb Stew, 116
   Kilarney Chowder, 46
   Old-Fashioned Beef Stew, 89
   Oxtail Soup, 33
   Paella, 135
   Split-Pea Soup, 38
   Vegetarian Sauce, 198
Pecans
   Orange-Cranberry Turkey
      Fettucine, 145
   Orange-Glazed Ginger
      Carrots, 175
   Peanut Butter Bread, 211
   Plantation Pork Chops, 105
   Pumpkin Nut Bread, 214
Peppercorns
   Greek Herbed Lamb with
      Rice, 114
Persimmons
   Persimmon Pudding, 202
   Tropical Bread with Brandy
      Hard Sauce, 212
Pesto
   Jalapeño Pesto, 36
Picante sauce
   Sausage Polenta Pie, 154
   Spicy Brisket over Noodles,
      66
Pine nuts
   Ground Turkey Vegetable
      Round, 153
   Mediterranean Caponata, 9

Touch of Green Soup with
   Goat Cheese Topping, 30
Tropical Bread with Brandy
   Hard Sauce, 212
Pineapple juice
   Hot Buttered Rum Punch, 18
   Soy-Glazed Spareribs, 98
   Tropical Tea, 19
Pineapple
   Curried Island Chicken, 133
   Hawaiian Pork Chops, 104
   Teriyaki Steak, 78
Pistachios
   Persimmon Pudding, 202
Pizza Beans, 165
Plantation Pork Chops, 105
Plum jelly
   Southeast Asian-style
      Meatballs, 150
Polenta
   Sausage Polenta Pie, 154
Pork & Lamb, 93–116
Pork
   Autumn Pork Chops, 102
   Barbecued Spareribs, 99
   Black Bean Chili with Pork,
      107
   Buck County's Spareribs, 97
   Chinese-style Country Ribs,
      97
   Corn-Stuffed Pork Chops,
      103
   Cranberry Pork Roast, 106
   Crockery Ham, 108
   Hawaiian Pork Chops, 104
   Indonesian Pork, 95
   Kiełbasa & Napa Cabbage,
      110
   Knockwurst with Hot
      German Potato Salad, 109
   North-of-the-Border Pozole,
      129
   Plantation Pork Chops, 105
   Rathskeller Pork, 101
   Rio Grande Country Ribs, 100
   Soy-Glazed Spareribs, 98
Pot roasts
   Black Forest Pot Roast, 57
   Favorite Pot Roast, 59
   New England Chuck Roast,
      90
   Pot Roast with Creamy
      Mushroom Sauce, 62
   Scandinavian Dilled Pot
      Roast, 63

Potatoes
    Favorite Pot Roast, 59
    Homestyle Short Ribs, 75
    Irish Lamb Stew, 116
    Knockwurst with Hot
        German Potato Salad, 109
    Old-Fashioned Beef Stew, 89
    Potato & Turnip Whip, 189
    Potato Soup, Florentine
        Style, 29
    Stuffed Potatoes, 187
Poultry, 117–154
Pretzels
    All-American Snack, 13
Prosciutto
    Sorrento Chicken Roll-ups,
        125
Prunes
    Algerian Lamb Shanks, 113
    Orange-Prune Compote, 235
Puddings
    Grandma's Rice Pudding,
        237
    Homestyle Bread Pudding,
        229
    Kahlua Bread Pudding, 220
    Persimmon Pudding, 202
    Traditional Plum Pudding,
        201
Pumpkin Nut Bread, 214
Pumpkin seeds
    Chicken Tortilla Casserole,
        130
Pumpkin
    Pumpkin Nut Bread, 214
    Sweet-Hot Pumpkin Soup, 35
Punch
    Bishop's Wine, 23
    Cranberry Wine Punch, 16
    Padre Punch, 17
    Spiced Apricot Punch, 16

R

Raisins
    Baked Apples, 236
    Curried Barley, 193
    Fresh Mango Chutney, 222
    Gar's Famous Mincemeat,
        231
    Grandma's Rice Pudding,
        237
    Nectarine Chutney, 221
    Shades of Autumn Rice, 196
    St. Helena Pears, 226
    Steamed Molasses Bread, 210

Traditional Plum Pudding,
    201
Tropical Bread with Brandy
    Hard Sauce, 212
Rathskeller Pork, 101
Red & Gold Sweet-Sour
    Chicken, 139
Red Beans & Rice, 157
Refried Bean Dip, 12
Refried Black Beans, 158
Rhineland Sweet-Sour Cabbage,
    173
Rhubarb
    Down-Home Rhubarb, 223
Ribs
    Barbecued Spareribs, 99
    Buck County's Spareribs, 97
    Chinese-style Country Ribs,
        97
    Rio Grande Country Ribs,
        100
    Soy-Glazed Spareribs, 98
Rice
    Arroz con Pollo, 127
    Beef Stroganoff, 91
    Caribbean "Jerked" Chicken,
        120
    Cashew Chicken, 119
    Chicken Breasts, Saltimbocca
        Style, 124
    Chili con Carne, 79
    Chinese Pepper Steak, 83
    Curried Island Chicken, 133
    Gingery Beef Strips, 87
    Grandma's Rice Pudding,
        237
    Greek Herbed Lamb with
        Rice, 114
    Jambalaya, 140
    Kowloon Chicken, 121
    Mexican Lamb with Red
        Wine, 115
    Paella, 135
    Red Beans & Rice, 157
    Shades of Autumn Rice, 196
    Swedish Cabbage Rolls, 73
    Turkey Fillets, Barbecue
        Style, 149
Rio Grande Country Ribs, 100
Rosy Cinnamon Applesauce,
    228
Rum
    Hot Buttered Rum Punch, 18
    Rum Sauce, 229
    Stuffed Honeyed Sweet

Potatoes, 186
Rye flour
    Blueberry Brown Bread, 213

S

Saffron
    Bouillabaisse, 49
Salads
    Fiesta Turkey & Bean Salad,
        161
    Knockwurst with Hot
        German Potato Salad, 109
Salsa
    Baja Beef 'n' Beans, 82
    Chicken Olé, 128
    Mexican Lamb with Red
        Wine, 115
    Rio Grande Country Ribs,
        100
Salt pork
    Favorite Baked Beans, 163
    Green Beans, Portuguese
        Style, 180
    New England Clam Chowder,
        48
    Savory Tomato Limas, 168
    Southwest Beef & Pintos,
        159
Sandwiches
    Barbecue Beef Sandwiches, 50
    Chili Dogs, 51
    Ham-Stuffed French Rolls,
        53
    Sloppy Jane Sandwiches, 51
    Sloppy Joes, 52
    Welsh Rarebit, 54
Sauces
    Brandy Hard Sauce, 212
    Hot Lime Sauce, 202
    Marinara Sauce, 197
    Rum Sauce, 229
    Spaghetti Meat Sauce, 72
    Vegetarian Sauce, 198
Sauerbraten
    Old World Sauerbraten, 61
Sauerkraut
    Buck County's Spareribs, 97
Sausage
    Chicken & Leek Terrine, 10
    Confetti Bean Casserole, 162
    Homestead Ham Loaf, 96
    Hot Sausage & Bean Stew,
        160
    Kielbasa & Napa Cabbage,
        110

Sausage (*continued*)
Knockwurst with Hot
German Potato Salad, 109
Paella, 135
Red Beans & Rice, 157
Sausage Polenta Pie, 154
Slow-Cooker Cassoulet, 170
Split-Pea Soup, 38
Savory Tomato Limas, 168
Scandinavian Dilled Pot Roast,
63
Sesame oil
Chicken Chop Suey, 132
Shades of Autumn Rice, 196
Shell Casserole, 71
Short ribs
German Short Ribs, 74
Homestyle Short Ribs, 75
Marco Polo Short Ribs, 76
Short-Cut Chili con Queso, 12
Short-Cut Turkey Chili, 152
Shrimp
Bouillabaisse, 49
Jambalaya, 140
Paella, 135
Sloppy Jane Sandwiches, 51
Sloppy Joes, 52
Slow cooking, 3
Slow-Cooker Cassoulet, 170
Slow-Cooker Fajitas, 64
Sorrento Chicken Roll-ups, 125
Soups & Sandwiches, 25–54
Soups
Bouillabaisse, 49
Congressional Bean Soup, 45
Down East Corn Chowder, 47
Fennel-Bean Soup, 27
French Onion Soup, 40
Georgia Peanut Soup, 34
Golden Squash Soup with
Pesto Topping, 36
Hamburger Soup, 31
Hearty Alphabet Soup, 37
Herbed Spinach Soup, 41
Kilarney Chowder, 46
Lentil Soup, Crescenti Style,
28
Minestrone Soup, 32
New England Clam Chowder,
48
Oxtail Soup, 33
Potato Soup, Florentine
Style, 29
Split-Pea Soup, 38
Swedish Cabbage Soup, 39

Tavern Soup, 42
Tortilla Soup, 43
Touch of Green Soup with
Goat Cheese Topping, 30
Turkey Noodle Soup, 44
Sour cream
Beef Stroganoff, 91
Hungarian Goulash, 81
Kilarney Chowder, 46
Rio Grande Country Ribs,
100
Shell Casserole, 71
Slow-Cooker Fajitas, 64
Sour Cream Limas, 167
Stuffed Potatoes, 187
Turkey Fillets, Barbecue
Style, 149
Southeast Asian-style Meatballs,
150
Southwest Beef & Pintos, 159
Soy sauce
Cashew Chicken, 119
Chinese Pepper Steak, 83
Chinese-style Country Ribs,
97
Gingery Beef Strips, 87
Indonesian Pork, 95
Southeast Asian-style
Meatballs, 150
Soy-Glazed Spareribs, 98
Teriyaki Steak, 78
Spaghetti Meat Sauce, 72
Spaghetti
Chicken Tetrazzini, 126
Spiced Apricot Punch, 16
Spices, 5
Spicy Brisket over Noodles, 66
Spicy Tomato Juice Cocktail,
21
Spinach
Fennel-Bean Soup, 27
Herbed Spinach Soup, 41
Potato Soup, Florentine
Style, 29
Split-Pea Soup, 38
Squash
Acorn Squash, Indonesian,
188
Autumn Pork Chops, 102
Golden Squash Soup with
Pesto Topping, 36
Herbed Squash Trio, 185
St. Helena Pears, 226
Steaks
Chinese Pepper Steak, 83

Creole-Asian Strips, 85
Flank Steak in Mushroom
Wine Sauce, 86
Gingery Beef Strips, 87
Stuffed Flank Steak with
Currant Wine Sauce, 88
Steamed Molasses Bread, 210
Stewed Pears with Ginger,
225
Stews
Farm-style Stew, 80
Flemish Carbonades, 60
Irish Lamb Stew, 116
Italian Meatball Stew, 70
North-of-the-Border Pozole,
129
Old-Fashioned Beef Stew, 89
Stirring, 3
Stroganoff
Beef Stroganoff, 91
Stuffed Flank Steak with
Currant Wine Sauce, 89
Stuffed Green Peppers, 184
Stuffed Honeyed Sweet
Potatoes, 186
Stuffed Potatoes, 187
Stuffed Turkey Breast, 146
Sun-dried tomatoes
Corn-Stuffed Pork Chops,
103
Party-style Ratatouille, 11
Vegetarian Sauce, 198
Venetian Chicken, 123
Swedish Cabbage Rolls, 73
Swedish Cabbage Soup, 39
Sweet potatoes
Stuffed Honeyed Sweet
Potatoes, 186
Sweet-Hot Pumpkin Soup, 35
Sweet-Sour Baby Onions, 182
Sweet-Sour Bean Trio, 166
Sweetened condensed milk
Homestyle Bread Pudding,
229
Swiss-style Beef Birds, 84

T

Tamale pie
California Tamale Pie, 67
Tarragon
Cornish Hens with Lime
Glaze, 142
Creole-Asian Strips, 85
Herbed Spinach Soup, 41

Tarragon (*continued*)
Tarragon Chicken Thighs, 138
Tavern Soup, 42
Tea
Tropical Tea, 19
Temperature switches, 5
Temperatures, 4
Teriyaki Steak, 78
Terrine
Chicken & Leek Terrine, 10
Thai Chicken, 136
Tomato sauce
Chicken Cacciatore, 122
Chicken Tortilla Casserole, 130
Eggplant-Artichoke Parmigiana, 179
Short-Cut Turkey Chili, 152
Spaghetti Meat Sauce, 72
Venetian Chicken, 123
Tomato soup
Savory Tomato Limas, 168
Stuffed Green Peppers, 184
Tomatoes
Calabacitas, 191
Couscous Provençal, 195
Creole Zucchini, 192
Green Beans, Portuguese Style, 180
Hot Sausage & Bean Stew, 160
Jambalaya, 140
Lentil Casserole, 194
Marinara Sauce, 197
Mock Chile Relleno, 178
Old-Fashioned Stewed Tomatoes, 190
Pizza Beans, 165
Red Beans & Rice, 157
Spaghetti Meat Sauce, 72
Spicy Tomato Juice Cocktail, 21
Tarragon Chicken Thighs, 138
Turkey Lasagna, 151
Vegetarian Sauce, 198
Tortillas
Beef Burritos, 58
Chicken Olé, 128
Chicken Tortilla Casserole, 130
Slow-Cooker Fajitas, 64
Tortilla Soup, 43
Touch of Green Soup with Goat Cheese Topping, 30

Touch-of-the-Orient Chicken Rolls, 131
Trade Winds Baked Custard, 239
Traditional Apple Butter, 238
Traditional Plum Pudding, 201
Tropical Bread with Brandy Hard Sauce, 212
Tropical Tea, 19
Turkey
Cran-Orange Turkey Roll, 147
Fiesta Turkey & Bean Salad, 161
Ground Turkey Vegetable Round, 153
Orange-Cranberry Turkey Fettucine, 145
Sausage Polenta Pie, 154
Short-Cut Turkey Chili, 152
Southeast Asian-style Meatballs, 150
Stuffed Turkey Breast, 146
Turkey Fillets, Barbecue Style, 149
Turkey Lasagna, **151**
Turkey Noodle Soup, 44
Turkey with Leek & White Wine Sauce, 148
Turnips
Old-Fashioned Beef Stew, 89
Oxtail Soup, 33
Potato & Turnip Whip, 189

U

Use & Care, 3–6

V

Vegetables & Side Dishes, 171–198
Vegetarian Sauce, 198
Venetian Chicken, 123
Vermouth
Cornish Hens with Lime Glaze, 142
Stewed Pears with Ginger, 225

W

Walnuts
Banana Nut Bread, 207
Blueberry & Orange Bread, 208
Chocolate Mint Dessert, 227

Cornish Hens with Lime Glaze, 142
Date & Nut Loaf, 215
Holiday Fruit Compote, 234
Shades of Autumn Rice, 196
Stuffed Honeyed Sweet Potatoes, 186
Traditional Plum Pudding, 201
Water chestnuts
Kowloon Chicken, 121
Touch-of-the-Orient Chicken Rolls, 131
Watercress
Kilarney Chowder, 46
Turkey with Leek & White Wine Sauce, 148
Welsh Rarebit, 54
Wine
Beef Burgundy, 77
Bishop's Wine, 23
Burgundy-basted Duckling, 143
Carrots in Dilled Wine Sauce, 174
Chicken Breasts, Saltimbocca Style, 124
Chicken Tetrazzini, 126
Cranberry Wine Punch, 16
Greek Herbed Lamb with Rice, 114
Hot Spiced Burgundy, 24
Marinated Leg of Lamb, 112
Mexican Lamb with Red Wine, 115
St. Helena Pears, 226
Stuffed Turkey Breast, 146
Turkey with Leek & White Wine Sauce, 148

Y

Yogurt
Black Bean Chili with Pork, 107

Z

Zucchini
Calabacitas, 191
Creole Zucchini, 192
Farm-style Stew, 80
Ground Turkey Vegetable Round, 153
Party-style Ratatouille, 11

Mable Hoffman

Mable Hoffman is a professional home economist and director of Hoffman Food Consultants. She concentrates her efforts on food consulting, food styling, recipe development and writing.

Included in Mable's writings are *Appetizers, California Cooking, Chocolate Cookery, Crepe Cookery, Deep-Fry Cookery, Ice Cream, Pasta in Minutes, Cookies in Minutes, Frozen Yogurt, Carefree Entertaining, Crockery Favorites* and *Tomatoes*. Her books have won four Tastemaker Awards, the "Oscar" for cookbooks, as best soft-cover cookbook of the year. Both *Crockery Cookery* and *Crepe Cookery* became #1 *New York Times* bestsellers.

Slow cooking is different and requires special recipes. Mable developed every recipe specifically for slow cookers. Mable's recipes invite culinary creativity. Just add a pinch of your own ingenuity to the pot. You'll find slow cooking makes good eating!